Contents

Written by LeeDell B. Stickler

2   Introduction
4   Resource Pak Contents

UNIT 1: New Life

5   Unit 1 Introduction
7   March 3
       1. Jesus Washes Feet
13   March 10
       2. The Passover Meal
19   March 17
       3. Praying in the Garden
25   March 24
       4. Palm Sunday
31   March 31
       5. The Resurrection
37   Unit 1 Reproducibles

UNIT 2: A New Paul

49   Unit 2 Introduction
51   April 7
       6. Paul's Conversion
57   April 14
       7. Down the Wall
63   April 21
       8. Lydia
69   April 28
       9. Paul and Silas
75   Unit 2 Reproducibles

UNIT 3: New Believers

85   Unit 3 Introduction
87   May 5
       10. The Community
           of Believers
93   May 12
       11. Peter and Cornelius
99   May 19
       12. Pentecost
105   May 26
       13. First Called Christians
111   Unit 3 Reproducibles

Supplemental Pages

122   New Life Cross
124   Cloaks and Branches (Unit 1, Session 4)
125   Comments from Users
126   Answers for the Bible Story Pak

This ladybug contains a hug or your special day. Mom, you're great! Let's celebrate! Happy Mother's Day!

Visit *GrowProclaimServe.com/leaders* to join the community with other leaders and find helpful weekly content and articles.

Cover Credits—Logo design: Marc Whitaker, MTWdesign; Background and frog: Shutterstock, Julien Tromeur; Cover design: Mark Foltz and Phillip D. Francis

Photo Credits: pp. 1, 8, 11, 14, 17, 23, 26, 29, 35, 61, 64, 67, 70, 88, 91, 97, 101, 109, 111, 114, 117, 118, 119, 122, 123: Ron Benedict; 113: Lisa Jackson

Art Credits: pp. 37-48, 75, 78, 79, 82, 119: Sharon Lane Holm/Storybook Arts, Inc.; pp. 56, 62, 68, 74, 91, 98, 103: Diana Magnuson/The Neis Group; pp. 83, 84, 120, 121: Shutterstock

Introduction

In the first unit (New Life), the boys and girls will hear the stories of Holy Week and Easter. Jesus and his friends were in Jerusalem to celebrate the Passover together. Passover was one of the three pilgrimage festivals of the Jewish faith. All people who could leave their villages and towns came to Jerusalem to observe the festival and all its fanfare at the Temple. It was during the Passover meal that Jesus announced to his friends what was about to happen in the coming days—how they would be called on to "remember him" and continue the spread of his message. As we tell these stories, we will be interpreting what "new life in Jesus" really means to a second or third grader, and how believing in Jesus changes everything about us from the inside out.

In the second unit (A New Paul), the children will meet Saul, who "spewed murderous threats" against the disciples of Jesus. They will see how his encounter with the risen Lord on the road to Damascus changed Saul's life forever. (Saul is better known by his Greek name "Paul." We will be using his Greek name in these stories so that it will not be confusing for the boys and girls, but you may want to mention that Saul and Paul are the same person.) In these stories we will also meet acquaintances of Paul—Ananias, who came to Saul's aid in spite of his better judgment; Lydia, who opened her household to him; and Silas, who learned that he could share the good news anywhere, even in jail.

In the third unit (New Believers), the boys and girls will hear "the rest of the story." What happened to the disciples after Easter? Did they just fade into the woodwork? Did they hide out, afraid of what would happen to them? They definitely did not. Jerusalem became dangerous for them, and many of the new believers set out for safer places to live. But wherever they went, they took the stories of Jesus with them. They effectively became the new church and kept Jesus' message alive. The children will learn who the first Christians were, how they lived, and where they got their name. Also in this unit, the children will engage with the rest of the faith community as they celebrate Pentecost—the birthday of the church.

Here at Grow, Proclaim, Serve, we feel it is important for the children not only to know the Bible stories, but also to apply the Bible message to their lives. In the third unit, the children are invited to be part of a mission to support the Kamina orphanage in the Democratic Republic of the Congo. The Kamina Project is an Advance Project of the General Board of Global Ministries of the United Methodist Church. The early Christians took seriously Jesus' teaching to "love your neighbor," and so do we.

Through this curriculum we want children to:
> grow in their relationships to God and to Jesus Christ;
> grow in discipleship;
> grow in their love of the Bible and in their Bible skills;
> grow in their relationships to one another; and
> grow to love their neighbors as themselves.

We want the children in this program to Grow in Faith, Proclaim the Word of God, and Serve God and neighbor. "Your faithfulness is growing by leaps and bounds, and the love that all of you have for each other is increasing." 2 Thessalonians 1:3

The Common English Bible

The CEB is the primary Scripture resource for Grow, Proclaim, Serve: Middle Elementary resources. Have at least one CEB in your room for the children to handle. We also recommend having a copy of the New Revised Standard Version and the Contemporary English Version of the Bible.

Grow, Proclaim, Serve: Middle Elementary resources are available in Braille on request.

Contact:

Braille Ministry,

c/o Donna Veigel

10810 N. 91st Avenue #96

Peoria, AZ 85345

(623-979-7552)

Grow, Proclaim, Serve: Middle Elementary, Bible Story Pak (one per child, one per leader)

The **Bible Story Pak** involves the children in the Bible story and provides them with a connection between the story and real life. The colorful activities are age-level appropriate, and **Stickers** for the attendance chart and other activities are included. Also included in the Story Pak is a music songbook.

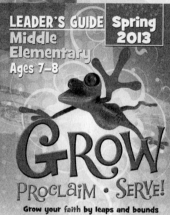

Grow, Proclaim, Serve: Middle Elementary, Leader's Guide (one per leader)

The **Leader's Guide** contains step-by-step instructions for each session. Leaders are encouraged to choose activities that best suit the needs of their children and the time available. At the front of each unit section is a list of the supplies that will be needed for those sessions. At the back of each unit section are reproducible pages that coordinate with the individual sessions in that unit.

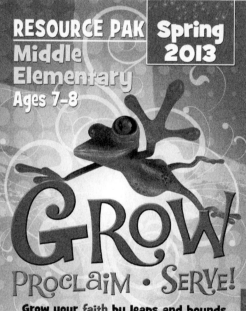

Grow, Proclaim, Serve: Middle Elementary, Resource Pak (one per group)

The **Resource Pak** contains Bible story posters, an attendance chart, and games that contribute to each session with the children. See page 4 for Resource Pak contents. Also included in the Resource Pak is an enhanced **CD-ROM** with the music for the quarter.

Included on the CD-ROM are vocal/instrumental and instrumental-only versions of each song, as well as printed music, word sheets, and PowerPoint® presentations for large groups. If you do not have access to a computer, the CD-ROM will play on a standard CD player. Track numbers for each song are provided in the Leader's Guide.

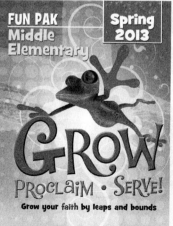

Grow, Proclaim, Serve: Middle Elementary, Fun Pak (one per child, one per leader)

The **Fun Pak** is a set of quick and easy craft activities that relate directly to each session. These activities are colorful, creative, and fun. They require few outside supplies and are aimed at the skill level of the middle elementary child.

Resource Pak Contents

Page	Sessions	Title
2, 23	1-13	Attendance Chart
3	1-5	Bible Story Poster Base (Unit 1)
4	1-13	Birthday Celebration
5, 7	1-5	Bible Story Poster Pictures (Unit 1)
9 (top)	6-9	Bible Story Poster Pictures (Unit 2)
9 (bottom)	10-13	Bible Story Poster Pictures (Unit 3)
12, 13	6-9	Bible Story Poster Base (Unit 2)
16	10-13	Bible Story Poster Base (Unit 3)
18	1-5	New Life Cross Strips
20	12-13	"I Will Serve Today" Game
21	1-5	How to Make the New Life Cross
22	10-13	Mission Poster

Using the Resource Pak

RESOURCE PAK Spring 2013
Middle Elementary
Ages 7–8

GROW
PROCLAIM • SERVE!

Grow your faith by leaps and bounds

- Remove the CD-ROM. It contains the music for the quarter. It can be played in a standard CD player. Track numbers are provided in the Leader's Guide. Print off a single copy of the music sheets and lyric sheets at the beginning of the quarter. Store in a folder.

- Remove the attendance chart and display it in a central location.

- Remove the story pictures for Unit 1 (pp. 5-7), punch them out, and store in an envelope. Display the poster (p. 3) in the worship area for Unit 1.

- Remove the pictures for the Unit 2 Poster (p. 9 [top]), and punch them out. Store until Unit 2.

- Remove the pictures for the Unit 3 Poster (p. 9 [bottom]), and punch them out. Store until Unit 3.

- Photocopy the directions for making the New Life Cross (p. 21) prior to Unit 1. Choose your method and prepare the cross before Session 1.

Unit I
New Life

Bible Verse

God so loved the world that he gave his only Son, so that everyone who believes in him won't perish but will have eternal life. (John 3:16)

Leap of Faith

God promises me new life through Jesus.

In this unit

Session 1	Session 2	Session 3	Session 4	Session 5
March 3	March 10	March 17	March 24	March 31
Jesus Washes Feet	*The Passover Meal*	*Praying in the Garden*	*Palm Sunday*	*The Resurrection*
Bible story:	Bible story:	Bible story:	Bible story:	Bible story:
John 13:1-15	Luke 22:14-23	Matthew 26:36-46	Mark 11:1-10	Matthew 28:1-10

CD-ROM

A New Life *(Track #1)*
- vocal and instrumental
- lead sheet
- lyrics
- PowerPoint® lyrics

This Is the Day *(Track #5)*
- vocal and instrumental
- lead sheet
- lyrics
- PowerPoint® lyrics

Leaper's Pointe (DVD)

Session 1

Jesus Washes Feet
It's "Cleanup-Roundup Day" in Leaper's Pointe, and everyone is helping. Because of Jesus' example, they start with the worst jobs and work their way up.

Session 2

The Passover Meal
Preparations are being made for dinner on the grounds with all our friends in Leaper's Pointe. It's the annual "Day to Remember," a time when each person in Leaper's Pointe remembers and appreciates something in her or his life.

Session 3

Praying in the Garden
Gabby is in her garden late at night, talking to God. The mayor comes out to make sure Gabby is all right. Gabby tells the mayor that she likes to talk to God at night and think of Jesus when he prayed in a garden.

Session 4

Palm Sunday
Mondo is directing the rehearsal for the annual Palm Sunday play. Things are not going so well—even the donkey is not cooperating! But Mrs. Finnanfeathers helps to change his mind.

Session 5

The Resurrection
Rosie can't believe Merrilee is not helping with the Easter egg hunt. Then Rosie and Farley realize Merrilee is reading the Bible passages that describe the Resurrection. They stop what they are doing and join Merrilee.

Leaper's Pointe in Concert (DVD)

- A New Life

Supplies

The Basics

CD player and/or DVD player
offering basket
scissors
markers (watercolor and permanent)
crayons
glue sticks

white glue
construction paper
colored copy paper
white copy paper
stapler, staples
paper punches
tape (clear, masking)
yarn/string
pencils

recycled newspaper
plastic drinking straws
lunch-sized paper bags
posterboard
rulers
plastic beads
chenille stems (a variety of colors)
wooden craft sticks

resealable plastic bags
wiggle eyes
ribbon (variety of widths)
cotton balls
cotton swabs
paper plates (variety of sizes and weights)

Beyond the Basics

Session 1
New Life Cross
1- by 5-inch strips of scrap paper
baking sheet with sides or shallow box lid
dirt/sand/pebbles
spray bottle
damp towel
bowl
pitcher
towels to sit on
large wiggle eyes
green copy paper
envelope

Session 2
New Life Cross
colored duct tape
disposable plastic table covers (54 x 108 inches)
memory game objects (see p. 15)
scarf (optional)
towels (optional)
bowl/napkins
charoset (see p. 16)
matzoh crackers
uncooked chicken egg
feathers
colored art foam (optional)
yellow and orange paper

Session 3
New Life Cross
flower bulb
yellow and green paper
green chenille stems

Session 4
New Life Cross
cardstock or cardboard
bamboo skewers
green copy paper
white crayons or chalk
green and blue crepe paper
yellow paper
royal blue copy paper

Session 5
New Life Cross
sunflower seeds or birdseed
3-inch wire ribbon

Tips

Sessions 1
All age levels are making a "New Life Cross." Choose one of the options provided on page 21 of the Resource Pak.

Session 2
Look on page 16 for an easy charoseth recipe so that the children can experience Passover first-hand.

Session 3
If the stickers' edges are beginning to peel up on the children's sit-upons, cover them with clear masking tape.

Session 4
Cut off the bamboo skewers' tips before making the Celebration Palm Branches to avoid any accidents.

Session 5
If you use sunflower seeds rather than birdseed for the Butterfly Shakers, you can staple the plates instead of using glue.

Reproducibles for Unit 1

These begin on page 37.

Jesus Washes Feet

Bible Verse

God so loved the world that he gave his only Son, so that everyone who believes in him won't perish but will have eternal life. (John 3:16)

Bible Story

John 13:1-15

Leap of Faith

God promises me new life through Jesus.

Before You Begin

Most people in Bible times, both male and female, wore sandals. They tied onto the foot using leather thongs, and the soles were made of wood or leather. There were no socks or stockings, so a person who regularly walked the streets of the city or countryside had extremely dirty feet. It was for this reason that people always removed their sandals on entering a house or any sacred place. It was the task of a servant to wash the grime from the feet of anyone who had come in from a journey. There was even a special basin designed with a foot rest for the procedure. Can you imagine a lowlier or more disgusting job?

Jesus and his friends had come to Jerusalem to celebrate the Passover. This was one of the three pilgrimage festivals in the Jewish religion. Every adult male was required to make the trip if he was physically able. Families often joined the men and made this a regular holiday. As our story begins, the disciples and Jesus had come together for the evening meal. Jesus took on the role of the servant since a servant had not been provided. With his actions, he demonstrated to his friends that he was not above doing the job of the lowliest servant.

When Jesus approached him, Peter protested loudly, feeling that this job was too degrading for Jesus. (He was also probably feeling a bit guilty.) But Jesus insisted on performing this task. If he didn't, then Peter (and the rest) would have no place with him (and what he was about to do). When Jesus returned to the head of the table, he pointed out that the disciples were to follow his example—serving, not being served. In order to be true followers, disciples of Jesus are called to be servants first, last, and always.

Children want to serve. But even now, the boys and girls have begun to decide which tasks are beneath them. They are particularly incensed when they have to clean up a mess that they didn't have any part in making, for example. But serving is the act of a true follower of Jesus. If Jesus washed dirt and grime off people's feet even though that wasn't his job, then we can help clean up a mess we didn't make, and we can do it with a joyful heart.

TIP

Visit *GrowProclaimServe. com/leaders* to join the community with other leaders and find helpful weekly content and articles.

Requires preparation.

Grow Together

Choose one or more of the following activities to do as the children arrive.

Welcome the Children

Supplies: **Resource Pak—pp. 2 & 23**, **Stickers**, **CD-ROM**, CD player, offering basket

- 🕐 Display the attendance chart from the Resource Pak.
- Play "A New Life" (Track #1) and "This Is the Day" (Track #5) as the children come into the room.
- Greet the children as they arrive.
- Show the children where to place their offerings.
- Give each child the attendance sticker for today to place on the chart.

Fun Pak Fun

Supplies: **Fun Pak—p. 3**, scissors, glue sticks, pencils, colored paper

- Have the children cut out and assemble the serving display stand.
- Then let them trace their handprints on colored paper and attach them to the stand.

Just for Fun

Supplies: **Bible Story Pak—p. 3**, crayons or markers

- The Bible Story Pak has four story and activity pages for each session. They are marked for the date. Remove the sheets for March 3. Give the children the Just for Fun page.
- Have the boys and girls color each ladybug with two spots on its back to discover the special word for today. *(Answer on p. 126.)*

Make Story Puppets

Supplies: **Reproducible 1a**, scissors, crayons or markers, scrap sheets of paper, clear tape

- 🕐 Photocopy enough finger puppets for each child to have one puppet. There are two puppets on the page—one male, one female. You may want to cut enough 1- by 5-inch strips of scrap paper for the class beforehand
- Follow the assembly instructions on the reproducible page, and use the Story Puppets during Conversation Time.

Conversation Time

Supplies: **Resource Pak—p. 4**, crayons or makers, tape, scissors, baking sheet with sides or shallow box lid, dirt, sand, pebbles, water, spray bottle, damp towel, Story Puppets (see above)

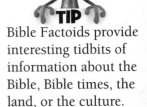

Bible Factoids provide interesting tidbits of information about the Bible, Bible times, the land, or the culture. These will relate to the Bible story.

🕐 Photocopy the birdhouse pattern and birthday gram for each child who has a birthday during this quarter.

- Bring the children together. They can sit around a table or on the floor. Give them a chance to briefly share any news of the week.

- Celebrate birthdays that have occurred or will occur in the coming week. Any child who has had a birthday or will have a birthday can write his or her name on a birdhouse and color it. Create a place on the wall for the birdhouses to be displayed. Also give those children the birthday gram ("Tweet the news! _____ has a birthday.") to color and take home.

- Set out the baking pan or box lid. Spread the dirt, sand, and pebbles in the tray.

SAY: Let's pretend that this is a Bible-times road. Whenever people in Bible times had to travel, they did it mostly on foot. Most of them could not afford a donkey or another pack animal. The roads, except for the main roads that were built by the Romans, were mostly dirt footpaths or cart trails.

- Invite each child to "walk" down the road using his or her finger puppet.

SAY: When it rained, these cart paths became a muddy mess. (*Spritz the tray with the water bottle and let the children walk down the road again.*)

ASK: What do you notice about the "feet" of your character? (*They became dirty.*) What kind of shoes did the people of Bible times wear? (*sandals*) What would you want to do before entering a house? (*take off my sandals*) Does removing the sandals remove all the dirt? (*No.*)

SAY: Even families who were not wealthy hired servants to wash the feet of guests who came to visit. There was even a special bowl with a footrest that they used. Nobody wanted to sit on dirty feet as they were eating. That's where our story for today begins. (*Wipe the children's fingers with the damp towel.*)

PRAY: Dear God, I thank you for these boys and girls. We are so glad they are here today. Help our faith to grow by leaps and bounds as we hear the Bible story and put the Bible message to work in our lives. Amen.

Proclaim the Word

Visit Leaper's Pointe

Supplies: DVD, DVD player

- The DVD is optional and can be used in place of "Interact With the Bible Story" or in addition to it.

- Place the DVD in the player. Locate Session 1.

- Invite the children to sit down where they can easily see the screen.

SAY: It's "Cleanup-Roundup Day" in Leaper's Pointe, and everyone is helping. They start with the worst jobs and work their way up. Want to know why? Because of Jesus' example. Jesus washed his disciples' feet to show how we should all serve one another.

- Watch the DVD segment.

Interact With the Bible Story

Supplies: Bible Story Pak—p. 1, low table with towels to sit on, bowl, pitcher, damp towel

SAY: Today's Bible story comes from the book of John in the New Testament of the Bible. John is one of the four Gospels that tell about the life of Jesus. *(Help the children locate John 13.)* Jesus was a great teacher. He not only told his disciples what they needed to know, but he also showed them what they were supposed to do.

* Have the boys and girls take off their shoes and sit around the table. Assign the parts and present the story from the Bible Story Pak. The person who takes on the role of Jesus can wipe the children's feet with the damp towel.

All About the Story

ASK: What did Jesus do for his disciples? *(He washed their feet.)* What did Peter do when Jesus came to him? *(He refused to let Jesus perform such a lowly task.)* How did Jesus respond? *(He said if Peter didn't let him wash his feet, then Peter could not have a place with him.)* After Jesus had performed this act of a servant, what did he tell his friends? *(He told them to follow his example.)*

SAY: Jesus was God's Son, but he was not so important that he could not serve others.

Countdown to Easter Lenten Calendar

Supplies: Bible, Bible Story Pak (first inside page & back cover), Stickers, scissors, resealable plastic bags

🕐 For each child, remove the first page from the Bible Story Pak and photocopy the "Read All About It!" list of Bible verses from the inside of the back cover. Cut out a set of the circular Lenten Calendar stickers for each child from the first sheet of stickers. (Keep the frog and yellow block stickers for other activities this week, and keep the attendance stickers for other sessions.)

* Give each child the calendar, the Bible verse list, a set of stickers, and a sandwich bag to hold his or her extra stickers until it's time to use them.

SAY: On March 31 we will celebrate Easter. Up until that day, we will learn things about Jesus and what he taught. Let's see how many days we have. *(28 days)*

* Locate the space on the calendar labeled March 3.

* Place the sticker that fits in that location, and read Luke 2:6-7.

SAY: Take this home with you today. On each day between now and Easter, add another sticker to the calendar and look up the Bible verse for that day. By the time Easter gets here, you will have completed the picture, and you will have read the stories of Jesus' life and Easter.

Bible Connection

Supplies: Bibles, Bible Story Pak—p. 4, Stickers, pencils

* The boys and girls will fill in the blanks about the story using their stickers and answer the questions about John 1:27. *(Answers on page 126.)*

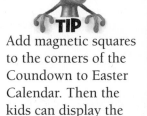

TIP

Add magnetic squares to the corners of the Coundown to Easter Calendar. Then the kids can display the calendar on their refrigerators.

Serve in Love

Kid Connection

Supplies: Bible Story Pak—p. 2, Stickers, felt-tip marker, white paper

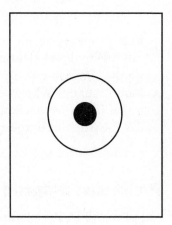

⏺ Draw a circle on a piece of white paper. Draw a smaller circle in the center of that circle and color it in with a black marker. (*See illustration.*)

ASK: (*Hold up the drawing.*) **What do you think this is?** (*Let the children guess.*)

SAY: It is a frog's egg. This is what a frog looks like when he begins his life. (*Look at Bible Story Pak—p. 2.*) As he grows into a frog, he changes. At each stage he is like a new creature. (*Talk about the changes shown in the illustration.*)

SAY: When we believe Jesus is God's Son, we try to live as Jesus taught us and to follow his example. When we do this, it changes how we act toward others.

ASK: What did Jesus try to show his disciples today? (*They should follow his example and serve others.*)

SAY: Jesus wanted his friends to know that being a disciple was more than just going around and learning stuff. It was about doing stuff, too. When we follow Jesus, we are called to "do stuff." When we do, it changes us.

- Have the children decide if the activities listed on the page are ways they are called to act. If so, have them place a frog sticker there.

Make a Frog for the New Life Cross

Supplies: Reproducible 1b, scissors, green copy paper, large wiggle eyes, white glue, crayons or markers (optional)

⏺ Photocopy the frog figure on green copy paper for each child. If green copy paper is not available, let the children color their frogs.

SAY: For the next four Sundays, we will be making animals or plants that grow into something that looks brand new. They change. This will remind us that as we grow, and as we learn more about Jesus and how to live as Jesus taught, the more how we act toward others also changes. We become like new on the inside.

- Have the children assemble the frog and bring it with them to worship. Remind the children to write their names on the backs so they can take them home after Easter.

Worship

Gather and Sing

Supplies: Bible Story Pak Songbooks, CD-ROM or DVD, CD player or DVD player, frog figures (see above), New Life Cross (see **Resource Pak—pp. 18 & 21**), tape

⏺ Choose one of the options to create a "New Life Cross" in the worship area. These can be found in the Resource Pak on page 21. Also see pages 122-23 in this Leader's Guide.

- Locate "A New Life" (Track #1) on the CD-ROM or DVD.

- Play the song through one time.

- Hand out the songbooks and let the children read through the words.

- Sing the song together.

SAY: Today we began hearing the stories about Jesus' last week on earth. We call it Holy Week. During this time we try to think about what we do and how we live. We ask ourselves: Is this what Jesus taught? Is this what Jesus would want me to do? When we live as Jesus taught, we change. Another way to say this is that Jesus gives us new life. When we follow Jesus, we do not change physically like the tadpole changing into a frog, but we change the way we act.

- The children will place their frog figures on the cross.

Praise and Respond

Supplies: Bible, Bible Story Pak Songbooks, Resource Pak—pp. 3, 5, & 7, Reproducible 1c, CD-ROM, CD player, envelope, tape

🕐 Display the Unit 1 Bible Story Poster Base. Remove the pictures for Sessions 1-5. Locate the story picture for Session 1 (*Jesus washing the disciples' feet*). Store the rest in an envelope for later sessions. Photocopy the movements for the song for each child.

TIP

Learn the dance moves (Reproducible 1c) so that you can teach them to the children.

- Play the song "This Is the Day" (Track #5) through one time.

- Read through the words together in the songbook. Hand out the pages with the movements to the song, and then teach the dance moves to the children.

- Play the song and move to the music.

SAY: On Easter Sunday we will celebrate the miracle that God performed. God raised Jesus from the dead. God gave Jesus new life. When we believe that Jesus is God's Son, God promises us new life, as well.

- Invite one of the children to read John 3:16.

- Then have one of the children place the picture from today's story on the poster with tape.

- Sing "This Is the Day."

PRAY: Dear God, we thank you for Jesus, who came into the world to teach us how we should live. Help us to follow his example in everything we do. Amen.

Plan for Next Week

Write-upon Sit-upons (p. 14): Photocopy **Reproducible 2a** for each child. Cut disposable plastic table covers into 15- by 30-inch rectangles, one for each child.

Interact With the Bible Story (p. 16): You may want to buy the matzoh crackers and make the charoset (recipe on p. 16) on Saturday night so that it will be fresh for Sunday.

Make an Egg and Chick for the New Life Cross (p. 17): Photocopy **Reproducibles 2b and 2c** for each child.

The Passover Meal

Bible Verse

God so loved the world that he gave his only Son, so that everyone who believes in him won't perish but will have eternal life. (John 3:16)

Bible Story

Luke 22:14-23

Leap of Faith

God promises me new life through Jesus.

Before You Begin

The celebration of Passover for the Jewish people is a festival of remembering. Every food they eat, every cup of wine they drink, every prayer they say is a way of remembering the time when God led their people out of slavery in Egypt. But the Passover celebration in today's story would be like none other.

Jesus, his friends, and their families had all gathered in that upper room in Jerusalem to eat the Passover meal. (Yes, the families were probably there.) After the meal was over, Jesus did something out of the ordinary. He took the cup and the bread from the meal and gave them a new meaning for the disciples. At first, the disciples appeared to be confused about what Jesus was trying to tell them. He said that he would be leaving them. But where was he going that they could not also go? He said that the coming times would be difficult. Why would the coming times be any *more* difficult than the times they were already experiencing? Why did Jesus want them to take strength in each other and in the things that they had done together? Why would they not turn to him for strength instead? How ironic it was that the person who led the guards to Jesus later that night was not a disgruntled member of the religious authorities, but one of Jesus' own inner circle who sat at the celebration table with them that very night.

Some churches include children in Holy Communion as soon as they are physically able to participate. Some churches wait until the children have a level of understanding of the sacrament. Others encourage the children to be "trained" before participating. It is true that the symbolism may be beyond their comprehension, but the event is a concrete way of saying, "I remember Jesus." That is just what Jesus wanted his friends to do and what we do today.

Talk with the children about what Jesus did that night and about some of the things the pastor says during the serving of Communion. Point out how the bread and the cup had great meaning for the Passover, and how they would now have meaning for the disciples in a different setting.

TIP

Visit *GrowProclaimServe. com/leaders* to join the community with other leaders and find helpful weekly content and articles.

Requires preparation.

Grow Together

Choose one or more of the following activities to do as the children arrive.

Welcome the Children

Supplies: Resource Pak—pp. 2 & 23, Stickers, CD-ROM, CD player, offering basket

⏰ Display the attendance chart from the Resource Pak.

- Play "A New Life" (Track #1) and "This Is the Day" (Track #5) as the children come into the room.

- Greet the children as they arrive.

- Show the children where to place their offerings.

- Give each child the attendance sticker for today to place on the chart.

Fun Pak Fun

Supplies: Fun Pak—p. 5, scissors, paper plates

- Have the children cut out the Passover food cards.

- Use one set of cards and invite a friend to play, or play "concentration solitaire."

Just for Fun

Supplies: Bible Story Pak—p. 3, Stickers

- The Bible Story Pak has four story and activity pages for each session. They are marked for the date. Remove the sheets for March 10. Give the children the Just for Fun page.

- Have the boys and girls use their stickers to fill in the events of Moses' life. (*Answers on page 127.*)

Write-upon Sit-upons

Supplies: Reproducible 2a, Stickers, scissors, colored duct tape, recycled newspaper, disposable plastic table covers (54 x 108 inches), permanent felt-tip markers

⏰ Cut the table covers into 15- by 30-inch rectangles, one for each child. One table cover will make nine sit-upons. Photocopy Reproducible 2a for each child.

- Assist the children as they tape the edges of their sit-upons.

- When the sit-upons are complete, have the children write their names in a decorative way. Then have them "autograph" their classmates' sit-upons.

- Have the children add the stickers for the stories of Holy Week to their sit-upons. You can add two stickers today (*Jesus washing the disciples' feet and the Passover meal*) and save the others for the following weeks, or add them all at once.

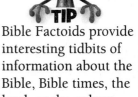

TIP

Bible Factoids provide interesting tidbits of information about the Bible, Bible times, the land, or the culture. These will relate to the Bible story.

GROW • **Proclaim** • **Serve** • Middle Elementary Leader's Guide

Conversation Time

Supplies: Birthday Celebration displays (see p. 8), crayons or markers, tape, scissors, up to 10 household objects, sit-upons (see p. 14), scarf (optional)

🕐 Identify each child who has a birthday this week and make sure you have a birdhouse pattern and birthday gram for him or her.

- Bring the children together. They can sit around a table or on the floor. If you made the sit-upons, let them sit on those. Give them a chance to briefly share any news of the week.

- Celebrate birthdays that have occurred or will occur in the coming week. Any child who has had a birthday or will have a birthday can write his or her name on a birdhouse and color it. Add it to the birdhouse display on the wall. Also give those children the birthday gram ("Tweet the news! _____ has a birthday.") to color and take home.

SAY: Let's see how good your memory is. (*Place the memory game objects on the table or floor where the children can easily see them.*) **Study these very carefully because I'm going to remove one or more objects. I want you to see if you can tell which have been taken away.**

- Have the children cover their eyes, then remove one or two objects.

ASK: Which objects did I remove? (*Whenever a child guesses correctly, he or she can remove the next object or objects.*)

SAY: In today's Bible story, we are still learning about the things that happened during Holy Week. Jesus and his friends have come to Jerusalem to celebrate the Passover, which is a holiday for remembering. God's people remember when Moses, with God's help, freed their ancestors from slavery in Egypt. (*Review the information the children filled in with stickers on the "Just for Fun" page.*) **In today's story Jesus gives his friends something new to remember and a way to do it.**

PRAY: Dear God, I thank you for these boys and girls. We are so glad they are here today. The Bible has so much to teach us about how God wants us to live. Help us to remember and put these teachings into action. Amen.

TIP

If your children have a tendency to peek, cover the objects with a scarf or piece of fabric as you remove some of them.

Proclaim the Word

Visit Leaper's Pointe

Supplies: DVD, DVD player

- The DVD is optional and can be used in place of "Interact With the Bible Story" or in addition to it.

- Place the DVD in the player. Locate Session 2.

- Invite the children to sit down where they can easily see the screen.

SAY: It's the annual "Day to Remember" in Leaper's Pointe—a time when each person remembers and appreciates something in her or his life.

- Watch the DVD segment.

Interact With the Bible Story

Supplies: Bibles, Bible Story Pak—p. 1, low table, sit-upons (see p. 14) or towels to sit on, bowl, charoset, matzoh crackers, napkins, hand sanitizer

SAY: Today's Bible story comes from the book of Luke in the New Testament of the Bible. Luke is one of the four Gospels that tell about the life of Jesus. *(Help the children locate Luke 22.)* As we learned last week, Jesus was a great teacher. He not only told his disciples what they needed to know, but he also showed them what they were supposed to do. In today's story, he gives his disciples a new way to remember him.

- Serve the charoset and matzoh crackers for the children to enjoy. They can dip their matzoh crackers into a common bowl, as Bible times people might have done. Be sure to ask if there are any children with food allergies!

- Assign the parts and present the story from the Bible Story Pak.

All About the Story

ASK: What did Jesus hint to his disciples? *(He would soon be leaving them.)* **What did he tell them to do whenever they ate the bread or drank the wine?** *(remember him)* **Who do you think is going to betray Jesus?** *(Judas)* **What is going to happen to Jesus that the disciples do not yet know about?** *(He will be crucified.)*

SAY: Jesus knew that his time on earth was short. He wanted his friends to continue the ministry that he had started.

Bible Connection

Supplies: Bible Story Pak—p. 4

- Have the boys and girls read about each item at the Passover meal and what it symbolizes for the Jewish people.

Pass the Passover Plate

Supplies: CD-ROM, CD player, paper plate, crayons or markers (optional)

🕐 Use a paper plate to represent the Passover meal. **OPTION: Create your own renditions of the Passover foods on the paper plate with crayons or markers.**

- Have the boys and girls sit in a circle. Begin passing the plate to the music.

- Whoever is holding the Passover plate when the music stops will tell something he or she remembers about Jesus—something he taught, something he did, or something that happened to him. Do this several times.

Serve in Love

Kid Connection

Supplies: Bible Story Pak—p. 2, Stickers, uncooked chicken egg

TIP

To make the charoseth: Grate 2 apples. Measure out 1 cup of grated apples and pour into a bowl. Add 1/2 cup of chopped walnuts and 1 teaspoon of cinnamon. Mix together, and then add enough grape juice to hold the mixture together (about 2 tablespoons).

ASK: *(Hold up the egg.)* **What do you think this is?** *(Let the children guess.)*

SAY: It is a chicken egg. This is what a chicken looks like when it begins its life.

ASK: What has to happen to make this egg become a clucking, walking, feathery chicken? *(A hen has to sit on it and give it time to develop.)* **When the chicken comes out of the egg, does it look like this?** *(Point to the adult chicken on the Bible Story Pak page.)* **No, of course not.** *(Talk about the changes shown in the illustration.)*

SAY: Just as the egg changes from this *(hold up the egg)* **to this** *(point to the adult chicken),* **when we try to live as Jesus taught us—to follow his example— it changes us, too. We act differently, and we treat others differently.**

ASK: What did Jesus try to show his disciples today? *(They were to remember him every time they ate the bread and drank the wine.)* **When we take Communion at church, what do you remember about Jesus?** *(Let the children contribute.)*

SAY: Being a disciple of Jesus is about doing stuff. It's also about remembering stuff about Jesus and what he taught.

- Have the children look at the statements on the Bible Story Pak page and see if they can remember the information about Jesus. They will use their stickers to fill in the words. *(Answers on page 126.)*

Make an Egg and Chick for the New Life Cross

Supplies: Reproducibles 2b & 2c, scissors, glue sticks, crayons or markers, colored art foam or colored copy paper (optional), feathers, tape, wiggle eyes, white glue, yellow and orange paper

🕐 Photocopy the patterns for the egg and chick and for the Easter storybook.

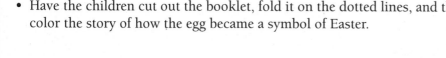

SAY: Between now and Easter we will be creating figures that represent "new life"—animals or plants that change as they grow. They change into something that looks brand new. This will remind us that as we grow, and as we learn more about Jesus and how to live as Jesus taught, we become like new on the inside. Last week we made frogs. Today we will make eggs and chicks.

- Have the children assemble the eggs and chicks and bring them to worship. Remind the children to write their names on the backs so they can take them home after Easter.

- Have the children cut out the booklet, fold it on the dotted lines, and then color the story of how the egg became a symbol of Easter.

Worship

Gather and Sing

Supplies: Bible Story Pak Songbooks, CD-ROM or DVD, CD player or DVD player, egg and chick figures (see above), New Life Cross (see p. 11), tape

- Locate "A New Life" (Track #1) on the CD-ROM or DVD.

- Play the song through one time.

- Hand out the songbooks and let the children read through the words.

- Sing the song together.

SAY: We are learning about what happened during Jesus' last week on earth. We call it Holy Week. As we hear these stories, we try to think about what we do and say and about how we live. When we live as Jesus taught, we change. Another way to say this is that Jesus gives us new life. When we follow Jesus, we do not change physically like the tadpole changing into a frog, or the egg turning into a chicken, but we change the way we act.

- The children will place their eggs and chicks on the cross.

OPTION: As the children place their figures on the New Life Cross, have them tell something about Jesus that they remember.

Praise and Respond

Supplies: Bible, Bible Story Pak Songbooks, Reproducible 1c, Unit 1 Bible Story Poster Base and Pictures (see p. 12), **CD-ROM**, CD player, tape

- 🕐 Locate the story picture for Session 2 (*Jesus and his disciples at the Passover meal*).
- Play the song "This Is the Day" (Track #5) through one time.
- Read through the words together in the songbook. Review the dance moves with the children.
- Play the song and move to the music.

TIP

Learn the dance moves (Reproducible 1c) so that you can teach them to the children.

SAY: On Easter Sunday we will celebrate the miracle that God performed. God raised Jesus from the dead. God gave Jesus new life. When we believe that Jesus is God's Son, God promises us new life, as well.

- Invite one of the children to read John 3:16.
- Then have one of the children place the picture from today's story on the poster with tape.
- Sing "This Is the Day."

PRAY: Dear God, we thank you for Jesus, who teaches us how we should live. When we celebrate Holy Communion, help us to remember what he taught and the things he did. Help us to follow his example in everything we do. Amen.

Plan for Next Week

Make Pocket Puppets (p. 20): Photocopy **Reproducible 3a** so that you have one Pocket Puppet pattern for each child. (There are two per page.)

Make a Daffodil for the New Life Cross (p. 23): Photocopy **Reproducible 3b** for each child.

Praying in the Garden

Bible Verse

God so loved the world that he gave his only Son, so that everyone who believes in him won't perish but will have eternal life. (John 3:16)

Bible Story

Matthew 26:36-46

Leap of Faith

God promises me new life through Jesus.

Before You Begin

After the Passover meal, Jesus and several of his followers left the city and went northeast to a garden on the Mount of Olives called Gethsemane. The garden may have been an olive grove owned by one of Jesus' followers. It also seems to be a place that Jesus and his friends had frequented at other times. This is why it was easy for Judas to lead the soldiers to the exact spot where they would find Jesus and arrest him.

In this quiet spot, away from the crowds of the city, Jesus prayed to God for a solution to the situation at hand. He knew what he was being asked to do, but he asked God one more time if there was *any other way* to accomplish God's purpose. But Jesus knew he would, in the end, do what God asked him to do. How sad it must have made him to find his trusted friends asleep instead of keeping watch as he had asked them to do; even sadder to know that one of his inner circle led the guards and crowd to his peaceful place of prayer.

Middle elementary boys and girls are reaching the age when their prayers can and should be more than "God bless Mommy and Daddy." Jesus was troubled in today's Bible story, and he instinctively turned to God. Boys and girls at this age are troubled by many things in their lives—things at school, things at home, things in their country, and things in the world. They often hear things they don't understand. At this point in their lives, teach them to turn to God. Ask intentionally for prayer requests during the conversation time or the closing worship. God will be there for them and will offer them a place to turn. God may not remove the trouble, but God will give them the strength to face whatever it is. God was there for Jesus. God will be there for them, too.

TIP

Visit *GrowProclaimServe. com/leaders* to join the community with other leaders and find helpful weekly content and articles.

Requires preparation.

Grow Together

Choose one or more of the following activities to do as the children arrive.

Welcome the Children

Supplies: Resource Pak—pp. 2 & 23, **Stickers, CD-ROM**, CD player, offering basket

Hearing the melodies and words of the songs, even as background music, will help the boys and girls learn the music. Music is a great teaching tool.

🕐 Display the attendance chart from the Resource Pak.

- Play "A New Life" (Track #1) and "This Is the Day" (Track #5) as the children come into the room.

- Greet the children as they arrive.

- Show the children where to place their offerings.

- Give each child the attendance sticker for today to place on the chart.

Fun Pak Fun

Supplies: Fun Pak—pp. 7-10, scissors, stapler, pencils

- Have the children cut out the prayer cards, Prayer Basket, and handle.

- Then have them assemble the basket and place the prayer cards inside.

Just for Fun

Supplies: Bible Story Pak—p. 3, pencils

- The Bible Story Pak has four story and activity pages for each session. They are marked for the date. Remove the sheets for March 17. Give the children the Just for Fun page.

- Have the boys and girls see how many times they can find the word *pray* in the word find puzzle. Then answer the question about prayer. *(Answers on page 127.)*

Make Pocket Puppets

Supplies: Reproducible 3a, scissors, crayons or markers, tape

🕐 Photocopy enough Pocket Puppets for each child to have one. There are two per page.

- Have the children assemble the puppets, and then save the puppets until it's time for the Bible story.

Conversation Time

Supplies: Birthday Celebration displays (see p. 8), sit-upons (see p. 14), tape, scissors, crayons or markers, paper

🕐 Identify each child who has a birthday this week and make sure you have a birdhouse pattern and birthday gram for him or her.

- Bring the children together. They can sit around a table or on the floor. If you made the sit-upons, let them sit on those. Give them a chance to briefly share any news of the week.

- Celebrate birthdays that have occurred or will occur in the coming week. Any child who has had a birthday or will have a birthday can write his or her name on a birdhouse and color it. Add it to the birdhouse display on the wall. Also give those children the birthday gram ("Tweet the news! _____ has a birthday.") to color and take home.

- Put two sheets of paper on the wall. At the top of one, write *Joys* and at the top of the other write *Concerns*.

SAY: Often in church the pastor asks for our "joys and concerns." Then these are included in the prayer. The pastor is thanking God for the joys in people's lives and asking for God's help with any concerns.

- Invite the children to suggest any "joys" and "concerns" they may have. Write them on the papers.

PRAY: Dear God, I thank you for these boys and girls. We are so glad they are here today. We thank you for *(include the joys that the children suggested)*. Dear God, we also need your help. *(Include the children's concerns.)* We know it isn't always in our best interests for you to make all our troubles just disappear, but we also know that you are here with us and will help us deal with anything. We trust that you know what's best for us. Thank you. Amen.

TIP

Group prayer should be very personal. Use the suggested prayer as a jumping-off point to make the prayer appropriate for your group.

Proclaim the Word

Visit Leaper's Pointe

Supplies: DVD, DVD player

- The DVD is optional and can be used in place of "Interact With the Bible Story" or in addition to it.

- Place the DVD in the player. Locate Session 3.

- Invite the children to sit down where they can easily see the screen.

SAY: Gabby is in her garden late at night, talking to God. The mayor comes out to make sure Gabby is all right, but Gabby tells the mayor that she likes to talk to God at night and think of Jesus when he prayed in a garden.

- Watch the DVD segment.

Interact With the Bible Story

Supplies: Bibles, Bible Story Pak—p. 1, Pocket Puppets (see p. 20)

SAY: Once again our Bible story comes from the New Testament of the Bible. It comes from the Book of Matthew. So far we have had stories from John, Luke, and Matthew. These books are called the Gospels because they help to tell the story of Jesus. *(Help the children locate Matthew 26.)* During Holy Week, we learn much about Jesus. We have learned what a great teacher he was, and how he not only told his disciples what he wanted them to do, he also showed them. In today's story, Jesus shows them that whenever he is troubled, he turns to God.

- Have the boys and girls put on their Pocket Puppets. Identify the disciple who is awake on one side and the one who is asleep on the other.

- Hold up the awake disciple and have the children copy you. Then turn the puppet to the other side with the sleeping disciple and make a snoring sound. Invite the kids to imitate.

- Then assign the parts and hear the story from the Bible Story Pak. When the disciples are awake, have the kids hold their puppets to the awake side. When they fall asleep, have them hold the puppets to the sleeping side and snore.

All About the Story

ASK: Why did Jesus go to the garden? *(to pray)* **What was troubling him?** *(He knew what was going to happen. He wondered if God could find another way.)* **What did he finally say to God?** *(Whatever you want me to do, I will do it.)* **What happened next?** *(Judas led the soldiers to the garden, and they arrested Jesus.)* **What do you think is going to happen next?** *(Let the children contribute.)*

SAY: God did not make all the troubles go away, even though Jesus asked. But God promised to be with Jesus through it all.

Bible Connection

Supplies: Bible Story Pak—p. 4, pencils

- Let the boys and girls identify which person or people each statement is indicating. Then they will draw a line to the picture of that person or those people. *(Answers on page 126.)*

Pray, Please!

SAY: When we pray, we often fold our hands and bow our heads and close our eyes. Did you know that this is not the only way to pray?

ASK: How would you pray if you were very joyful? *(Invite the children to act out their answers. After each type of prayer, have the children position their bodies in a way that would reflect that kind of prayer.)* **How would you pray if you were very sad? How would you pray if you were asking God for something very, very special? How would you pray if you were feeling very quiet and thoughtful?**

SAY: In the Bible we hear stories about how God's people talked to God not only with their voices, but also with their bodies. The most important thing is that we talk to God.

Serve in Love

Kid Connection

Supplies: Bible Story Pak—p. 2, Stickers, sit-upons (see p. 14), flower bulb, pencils

ASK: *(Hold up the flower bulb.)* **What do you think this is?** *(Let the children guess.)* It is a flower bulb. What kind of a flower do you think it is? It doesn't look much like a flower right now, does it? What has to happen to make this bulb become a flower? (*It has to have good soil, water, sunshine, and time. Talk about the changes shown in the Bible Story Pak illustration.*)

SAY: Just as the flower bulb changes from this (*hold up the bulb*) to this (*point to the flower*), when we try to live as Jesus taught us—to follow his example—it changes us, too. We grow to be a different kind of person than if we did not know Jesus.

ASK: What did Jesus show his disciples today? (*When they were troubled, they could turn to God in prayer.*) **Do you pray?** (*Let the children contribute.*) **When do you pray?**

SAY: Being a disciple of Jesus is about doing stuff. One of the things Jesus wants his disciples to do is talk to God.

- Invite the children to fill in possible things to pray in each of the listed settings on the Bible Story Pak page.

- If you made the sit-upons and are adding a sticker for each story, add the picture of Jesus praying today.

Make a Daffodil for the New Life Cross

Supplies: Reproducible 3b, scissors, glue sticks, yellow and green paper, green chenille stems, paper punches, tape, crayons or markers (optional)

🕐 Photocopy the daffodil patterns for each child.

SAY: Between now and Easter we will be creating figures that represent "new life"—animals or plants that change as they grow. They change into something that looks brand new. This will remind us that as we grow, and as we learn more about Jesus and how to live as Jesus taught, we become like new on the inside. We've made frogs and eggs and chicks. Today we will make a daffodil, a beautiful spring flower that comes from a bulb.

- Have the children assemble the daffodil and bring it with them to worship. Remind the children to write their names on the backs so they can take them home after Easter.

TIP
If the edges of the stickers are curling up or having difficulty sticking to the plastic, use clear masking tape to hold them down.

Worship

Gather and Sing

Supplies: Bible Story Pak Songbooks, CD-ROM or DVD, CD player or DVD player, daffodil figures (see above), New Life Cross (see p. 11), tape

- Locate "A New Life" (Track #1) on the CD-ROM or DVD.

- Play the song through one time.

- Hand out the songbooks and let the children read through the words.

- Sing the song together.

SAY: We are learning about what happened during Jesus' last week on the earth. We call it Holy Week. As we hear these stories, we try to think about what we do and say and about how we live each day. We ask ourselves: Is this what Jesus taught? Is this what Jesus would want me to do? We know that when we live as Jesus taught, we change. This is another way to say that Jesus gives us new life. When we follow Jesus, we do not change physically like the tadpole changing into a frog, the egg turning into a chicken, or the bulb turning into a flower; but we change the way we act, the things we do, and the way we treat other people.

- The children will place their daffodils on the cross.

Praise and Respond

Supplies: Bible, Bible Story Pak Songbooks, Reproducible 1c, Unit 1 Bible Story Poster Base and Pictures (see p. 12), CD-ROM, CD player, tape

🕐 Locate the story picture for Session 3 (*Jesus praying in the garden*).

- Play the song "This Is the Day" (Track #5) through one time.
- Review the dance moves with the children.
- Then play the song and move to the music.

SAY: On Easter Sunday we will celebrate the miracle that God performed. God raised Jesus from the dead. God gave Jesus new life. When we believe that Jesus is God's Son, God promises us new life, as well.

- Invite one of the children to read John 3:16.
- Then have one of the children place the picture from today's story on the poster with tape.
- Sing "This Is the Day."
- Invite the children to suggest any joys or concerns they would like to include in the closing prayer.

PRAY: Dear God, we thank you for Jesus, who came into the world to teach us how to live. We are glad that we can turn to you in prayer. (*Include any joys and concerns here.*) Help us to follow Jesus' example in everything we do. Amen.

Plan for Next Week

Fun Pak Fun (p. 26): Photocopy the diorama background (**Fun Pak—p. 12**) on white copy paper, one for each child. Cut an eight-inch square of cardstock or cardboard for each base.

Make Celebration Palm Branches (p. 26): Photocopy **Reproducible 4a** on green copy paper, two copies per child. Cut the tips off of bamboo skewers, one per child.

Cloaks and Branches (p. 28): Photocopy **p. 124** for every four children. (Each pair of children will need one cloak and one branch.) Cut out the pictures and glue each one to a different sheet of construction paper or scrap copy paper.

Make a Peacock for the New Life Cross (p. 29): Photocopy **Reproducible 4b** on royal blue copy paper for each child.

Palm Sunday

Bible Verse

God so loved the world that he gave his only Son, so that everyone who believes in him won't perish but will have eternal life. (John 3:16)

Bible Story

Mark 11:1-10

Leap of Faith

God promises me new life through Jesus.

Before You Begin

The stories of Jesus' last week on earth are some of the foundational stories of our Christian faith. It is hard to imagine that so much happened in one short week. Jesus comes to Jerusalem for the Passover, he is arrested in the garden of Gethsemane, he is tried before the Sanhedrin, and finally, before Pilate himself. Then he is crucified and buried.

Today, Palm Sunday, is the day that set all of the other days in motion. Up until this time, Jesus had focused his ministry on the area of Galilee, remaining discreetly out of the city of Jerusalem. He knew that to confront the Jewish religious leaders on their own turf would cause trouble. And indeed it did. But it was trouble that God had already foreseen and trouble that was necessary for God's purpose to be fulfilled.

All four Gospels tell the story of Jesus' entry into Jerusalem. Each one varies slightly, but we know that the people greeted Jesus joyfully as the king they thought he was. They called upon him to "save us" (which is what *hosanna* means). What the people actually had in mind, however, was for Jesus, as the promised Messiah, to rid them of the Roman domination. They thought that Jesus was a military Messiah. We know, however, that this was not God's purpose for sending Jesus. This massive display of adoration, however, made the religious authorities nervous. They hoped that the Roman officials would not take this as an opportunity to come down on them too harshly.

The stories of Holy Week and Easter are much harder to tell than the stories of Christmas or the life of Jesus. They involve deceit, betrayal, cowardice, greed, and other not-so-admirable character traits. But hearing these stories helps the children understand the great gift that God gave to us through Jesus Christ. God was able to overcome all that Jesus had to endure. "Hosanna! Blessings on the one who comes in the name of the Lord!"

TIP

Visit *GrowProclaimServe.com/leaders* to join the community with other leaders and find helpful weekly content and articles.

Requires preparation.

Grow Together

Choose one or more of the following activities to do as the children arrive.

Welcome the Children

Supplies: Resource Pak—pp. 2 & 23, Stickers, CD-ROM, CD player, offering basket

- Display the attendance chart from the Resource Pak.
- Play "A New Life" (Track #1) and "This Is the Day" (Track #5) as the children come into the room.
- Greet the children as they arrive.
- Show the children where to place their offerings.
- Give each child the attendance sticker for today to place on the chart.

Hearing the melodies and words of the songs, even as background music, will help the boys and girls learn the music. Music is a great teaching tool.

Fun Pak Fun

Supplies: Fun Pak—pp. 11-12, scissors, glue sticks, cardstock or cardboard, crayons or markers, rulers

- Photocopy the diorama background (**Fun Pak—p. 12**) on white copy paper, one for each child. Cut an 8-inch square of cardstock or cardboard for each base.
- Have the children cut out and color the diorama background. Let them assemble it and glue it to the base.
- Assemble the figures and place them in the diorama to tell the story of Palm Sunday.

Just for Fun

Supplies: Bible Story Pak—p. 3, pencils

- The Bible Story Pak has four story and activity pages for each session. They are marked for the date. Remove the sheets for March 24. Give the children the Just for Fun page.
- Have the children circle every other letter on the path to discover what the people shouted as Jesus rode into Jerusalem. (*Answer on page 126.*)

Make Celebration Palm Branches

Supplies: Reproducible 4a, green copy paper, scissors, bamboo skewers, glue sticks, tape, crayons or markers (optional)

- Photocopy the palm leaf pattern onto green paper. If green paper is not available, provide green crayons or markers so the children can color their leaves. Each child will need two. Cut off the sharp tip of each bamboo skewer to avoid any accidents.
- Have each child cut out two palm leaves.
- Then they will tape a skewer to the back side of one of the palm leaves, leaving about 5 inches extending below the leaf as shown here. The tape

makes sure the stick won't slip as the child waves it.

- Put glue on the second palm leaf and lay it on top of the first, sandwiching the stick between the two leaves. Press along the stick.

- Snip along the solid lines from the outer edges to the center, stopping before getting to the stick.

- Save these for use during the Bible story time.

Conversation Time

Supplies: Birthday Celebration displays (see p. 8), sit-upons (see p. 14), tape, scissors, crayons or markers

🕐 Identify each child who has a birthday this week and make sure you have a birdhouse pattern and birthday gram for him or her.

- Bring the children together. They can sit around a table or on the floor. If you made the sit-upons, let them sit on those. Give them a chance to briefly share any news of the week.

- Celebrate birthdays that have occurred or will occur in the coming week. Any child who has had a birthday or will have a birthday can write his or her name on a birdhouse and color it. Add it to the birdhouse display on the wall. Also give those children the birthday gram ("Tweet the news! _____ has a birthday.") to color and take home.

ASK: Have you ever been to a parade? What was it like? What were you celebrating? *(Let the children contribute.)*

SAY: Parades are exciting. There is usually music and shouting for joy. There are bands, floats, and banners. Today's Bible story tells about a special parade. This parade was fun, too, but not everyone in Jerusalem was celebrating.

- Invite the children to suggest any "joys" and "concerns" they may have. Make this an integral part of your opening prayers.

PRAY: Dear God, I thank you for these boys and girls. We are so glad they are here today. We thank you for *(include the joys that the children suggested)*. **Dear God, we also need your help.** *(Include the children's concerns.)* **Today is Palm Sunday—a very special day in our church. We celebrate Jesus, just as the people in Jerusalem celebrated him many, many years ago. We are so glad that he lived among us and helped us to know you better. Amen.**

TIP

Continue to ask about joys and concerns each week during this personal time with the children.

Proclaim the Word

Visit Leaper's Pointe

Supplies: DVD, DVD player

- The DVD is optional and can be used in place of "Interact With the Bible Story" or in addition to it.

- Place the DVD in the player. Locate Session 4.

- Invite the children to sit down where they can easily see the screen.

SAY: Mondo is directing the rehearsal for the annual Palm Sunday play. Things are not going so well—even the donkey is not cooperating! Mrs. Finnanfeathers talks to the donkey as Mondo tells the story of Jesus' triumphal entry into Jerusalem.

- Watch the DVD segment.

Interact With the Bible Story

Supplies: Bibles, Bible Story Pak—p. 1, Celebration Palm Branches (see p. 26)

SAY: Today is the beginning of Holy Week in our church. It all begins on Palm Sunday. It's hard to imagine that so many things happened in one short week. Jesus came to Jerusalem. Jesus ate the Passover meal with his friends. Jesus was arrested while he was praying. He was tried in the court, he was put to death on a cross, and on the third day, guess what happened? (*Let the children add: God raised him from the dead.*)

- Assign the parts and hear the story from the Bible Story Pak. When it comes time for the entry into the city, let all the children wave their palm branches.

All About the Story

ASK: Why did Jesus come to Jerusalem? (*He came to celebrate the Passover.*) **How did the people greet him?** (*They greeted him joyfully, as though he were a king.*) **What was he riding on?** (*He rode a donkey.*) **Why was this important?** (*The prophets said that a king would come to the people riding on a donkey.*) **Do you think the religious authorities in the city were glad to see Jesus?** (*No, probably not.*)

SAY: Many of the religious authorities didn't like Jesus. He was always telling people one thing when their laws said the people should do something different. This was a special time—Passover—and they didn't want anything to disturb the peace. And to them, Jesus was a troublemaker.

Bible Connection

Supplies: Bible Story Pak—p. 4, pencils

- Let the boys and girls put the missing words on the lines and then into the puzzle. When they do, they will discover a special word. (*Answers on page 126.*)

Cloaks and Branches

Supplies: Leader's Guide—p. 124, scissors, construction paper or scrap copy paper, glue

🕐 Photocopy the cloak and palm branch patterns. Each pair of children will need one cloak and one branch. Cut them out and glue each one to a sheet of construction paper (or scrap copy paper).

- Divide the children into teams of two. One child will be Jesus, and the other will be a crowd member.

- The crowd member will place either the cloak or the palm branch on the floor and the child representing Jesus will step on it. Then the crowd member will place the other picture on the floor and Jesus will step forward.

- Continue until Jesus has reached a designated spot in the room. The first team to get there wins.

Serve in Love

Kid Connection

Supplies: Bible Story Pak—p. 2, Stickers, sit-upons (see p. 14)

ASK: *(Hold up the Bible Story Pak page.)* **What bird is pictured in our New Life Connection for this week?** *(It's a peacock.)* **How do you think a peacock is a symbol of new life?** *(Let the children contribute.)*

SAY: **Most people think of the peacock as a symbol of vanity and pride because the male struts around with his beautiful tail, showing off for the lady peahens. But early Christians thought of the peacock as a symbol of new life, because every year the peacock loses its tail and then grows another one back—one that is even prettier than before.**

SAY: **On Palm Sunday the people celebrated Jesus as he came into Jerusalem. We can celebrate Jesus, too, by the things we do each day.**

- Invite the children to place a palm branch sticker next to each activity that is a way we can celebrate Jesus in our lives today.

- If you made the sit-upons and are adding a sticker for each story, add the picture of Jesus arriving in Jerusalem.

TIP

If the edges of the stickers are curling up or having difficulty sticking to the sit-upon, use clear masking tape to hold them down.

Make a Peacock for the New Life Cross

Supplies: Reproducible 4b, Stickers, scissors, tape, white crayons or chalk, green and blue crepe paper, glue sticks, yellow paper, royal blue copy paper, rulers, crayons or markers (optional)

🕐 Photocopy the peacock body onto royal blue copy paper. If this is not available, allow the children to simply color their peacocks.

SAY: **The peacock reminds us that as we learn more about what Jesus taught, we shed some of our old behaviors and begin to live as Jesus taught. When we do this, we have new life on the inside.**

- Have each child assemble a peacock and bring it to worship. Remind the children to write their names on the backs so they can take them home after Easter.

Worship

Gather and Sing

Supplies: Bible Story Pak Songbooks, CD-ROM or DVD, CD player or DVD player, peacock figures (see above), New Life Cross (see p. 11), tape

- Locate "A New Life" (Track #1) on the CD-ROM or DVD.

- Hand out the songbooks for any children who need help remembering the words.

- Play the song and let the children sing it together.

SAY: We are learning about what happened during Jesus' last week on earth. We call it Holy Week. As we hear these stories, we try to think about what we do and say and about how we live. We ask ourselves: Is this what Jesus taught? Is this what Jesus would want me to do? We know that when we live as Jesus taught, we change. This is another way to say that Jesus gives us new life. When we follow Jesus, we do not change physically like the tadpole changing to a frog, the egg turning into a chicken, the bulb turning into a flower, or the peacock growing new tail feathers; but we change the way we act, the things we do, and the way we treat other people.

- The children will place their peacocks on the cross.

Praise and Respond

Supplies: **Bible, Bible Story Pak Songbooks, Reproducible 1c, Unit 1 Bible Story Poster Base and Pictures** (see p. 12), **CD-ROM,** CD player, tape

- Locate the story picture for Session 4 (*Jesus entering Jerusalem*).

- Review the dance moves to "This Is the Day" (Track #5). Sing and move to the music.

SAY: Next Sunday is Easter Sunday. This is the day we celebrate Jesus' resurrection. God raised Jesus from the dead. God gave Jesus new life. When we believe that Jesus is God's Son, God promises us new life, as well.

- Invite one of the children to read John 3:16.

- Then have one of the children place the picture from today's story on the poster with tape.

- Sing "This Is the Day."

- Invite the children to suggest any joys or concerns they would like to include in the closing prayer.

PRAY: Dear God, we thank you for Jesus, who came into the world to teach us how to live. We celebrate Jesus and all that he said and did. Help us to celebrate him with the ways we choose to live every day. Amen.

Plan for Next Week

Make Butterfly Shakers (p. 32): Photocopy **Reproducible 5a** for each child.

Make a Butterfly for the New Life Cross (p. 35): Photocopy **Reproducible 5b** for each child. Try to find three-inch-wide wire ribbon for this activity.

The Resurrection

Bible Verse

God so loved the world that he gave his only Son, so that everyone who believes in him won't perish but will have eternal life. (John 3:16)

Bible Story

Matthew 28:1-10

Leap of Faith

God promises me new life through Jesus.

Before You Begin

Jesus died the death not of a king, but of a criminal. In fact, Jesus shared his death with sinners, just as he had often spent time with them during his life. He was crucified on a Friday afternoon, and since the Jewish Sabbath begins at sundown, it was imperative that his body be buried before then since it is not lawful to bury the dead on the Sabbath. So Jesus was placed in the borrowed tomb of Joseph of Arimathea. Joseph was a secret disciple of Jesus, and he had gone to Pilate and asked permission to bury the man from whom he had learned so much.

Because everything had been done in such a hurry, the women followers came to the garden to complete the burial process after the Sabbath was over. (In the story of the Resurrection told in the Book of Matthew, there are two women: Mary Magdalene and the "other Mary.") They wanted to anoint Jesus' body with spices, myrrh, and aloes. What they found when they got there, however, was totally unexpected. The events of the morning began with an earthquake and ended with the resurrected Christ, who instructed them to tell the others. Jesus was alive and would go to Galilee and meet them there.

Easter is the highlight of the Christian year, a day of great rejoicing. Jesus is alive! We serve a risen Savior. After the time of great sadness, the world is once again made right. Focus on the joy. Set a mood of celebration and happiness in the room.

Children may have many questions about the Resurrection. Answer them as simply and as honestly as possible. As adults, we still don't have all the answers. It is also appropriate to tell the children that you do not know, but that you trust in God and believe that God can do anything. Our Savior is a risen Savior and is alive and well and in the world today. Amen!

Session 5
March 31

TIP

Visit *GrowProclaimServe. com/leaders* to join the community with other leaders and find helpful weekly content and articles.

Requires preparation.

Grow Together

Choose one or more of the following activities to do as the children arrive.

Welcome the Children

Supplies: **Resource Pak—pp. 2 & 23, Stickers, CD-ROM**, CD player, offering basket

TIP
Hearing the melodies and words of the songs, even as background music, will help the boys and girls learn the music. Music is a great teaching tool.

🕐 Display the attendance chart from the Resource Pak.

- Play "A New Life" (Track #1) and "This Is the Day" (Track #5) as the children come into the room.

- Greet the children as they arrive.

- Show the children where to place their offerings.

- Give each child the attendance sticker for today to place on the chart.

Fun Pak Fun

Supplies: **Fun Pak—p. 13**, scissors, tape, small paper plates, chenille stems, pencils, glue sticks, wiggle eyes

- Have the children cut out the pedestal base, the Bible verse circle, and the butterfly.

- Glue the Bible verse circle to the paper plate, and follow the assembly instructions.

Just for Fun

Supplies: **Bible Story Pak—p. 3**, pencils

- The Bible Story Pak has four story and activity pages for each session. They are marked for the date. Remove the sheets for March 31. Give the children the Just for Fun page.

- Have the boys and girls use the butterfly code to discover what the women found at the tomb on that special morning. (*Answer on page 126.*)

Make Butterfly Shakers

Supplies: **Reproducible 5a**, scissors, crayons or markers, glue sticks, white glue or stapler/staples, two 6-inch paper plates per child, sunflower seeds or birdseed

🕐 Photocopy the butterfly circles, one page for each child. (There are two butterfly circles per page.)

- Have each child cut out and color the two butterflies. Glue one to the bottom side of each paper plate with glue stick.

- Put a scoop of the sunflower seeds or bird seed in the center of one plate.

- Run a line of white glue around the plate's edge and place the other on top with the butterfly facing out. (**Hint:** You can staple if you use sunflower seeds.)

- Have the children shake their butterflies every time you say: **Jesus is alive.** Do this frequently and at unexpected times so that the children can get into the joy of the day. Later, have the children bring their shakers to worship.

Conversation Time

Supplies: Birthday Celebration displays (see p. 8), sit-upons (see p. 14), tape, scissors, crayons or markers, Butterfly Shakers (see p. 32)

🕐 Identify each child who has a birthday this week and make sure you have a birdhouse pattern and birthday gram for him or her.

- Bring the children together. They can sit around a table or on the floor. If you made the sit-upons, let them sit on those. Give them a chance to briefly share any news of the week.

- Celebrate birthdays that have occurred or will occur in the coming week. Any child who has had a birthday or will have a birthday can write his or her name on a birdhouse and color it. Add it to the birdhouse display on the wall. Also give those children the birthday gram ("Tweet the news! _____ has a birthday.") to color and take home.

SAY: Jesus is alive! *(Pause for the children to shake their butterflies.)*

ASK: What is so special about Jesus being alive? Aren't you alive? Aren't I alive? *(Invite the children to come up with the answer that God raised Jesus from the dead.)*

SAY: That's what makes this day so very special. This had never happened before—ever. That is why we are celebrating.

- Invite the children to suggest any "joys" and "concerns" they may have. Make this an integral part of your opening prayers.

PRAY: Dear God, today is such a wonderful day. We can't possibly imagine how Jesus' disciples felt that morning when they discovered that Jesus was alive. *(Some children may shake their butterflies at this point. That's OK.)* No one is more powerful than you are. You are stronger than death, and because we believe that Jesus is your Son, you have promised us new life, too. Thank you for *(include the joys that the children suggested)*. And please help with *(include the children's concerns)*. Amen. Jesus is alive!

TIP

Continue to ask about joys and concerns each week during this personal time with the children.

Proclaim the Word

Visit Leaper's Pointe

Supplies: DVD, DVD player

- The DVD is optional and can be used in place of "Interact With the Bible Story" or in addition to it.

- Place the DVD in the player. Locate Session 5.

- Invite the children to sit down where they can easily see the screen.

SAY: Rosie and Farley are busy hiding eggs for the Easter egg hunt and Mondo is practicing his lines for the Easter play when the mayor calmly comes out of her house, spreads out a blanket, and sits down to read. Rosie can't believe that Merrilee is not helping, but then Rosie and Farley realize that Merrilee is reading the Bible passages that describe the Resurrection. They stop what they are doing and join Merrilee. Mondo soon joins them, as well. They all remind us that Easter is not about egg hunts, bunnies, or even Easter plays—it is about the good news that Jesus is alive!

• Watch the DVD segment.

Interact With the Bible Story

Supplies: Bible Story Pak—p. 1, Butterfly Shakers (see p. 32)

SAY: Holy Week is over. It began with Palm Sunday and ended with Jesus being put to death on the cross. But now three days have passed. No one suspected what was going to happen that morning—least of all the two women who came to the garden to prepare Jesus' body for a proper burial.

• Assign the parts and hear the story from the Bible Story Pak. Whenever the phrase "Jesus is alive" is said, encourage the children to shake their butterflies.

All About the Story

ASK: What time of day did Mary Magdalene and the other Mary come to the garden? *(dawn)* Why? *(They wanted to be there before anyone else was up and moving.)* What did they find when they got there? *(an angel sitting on top of the stone door)* What did the angel look like? *(white and shiny)* What did the angel tell them? *(God has raised Jesus from the dead. Jesus is alive.)* Who else did they see? *(Jesus)* What did Jesus tell them? *(Go tell the others. He'll see them in Galilee.)*

SAY: What an exciting morning! No one ever expected what the women found. Jesus had told them, but they had not believed. Now it was true. Jesus is alive!

Bible Connection

Supplies: Bible Story Pak—p. 4, pencils

• Have the boys and girls connect the dots and discover two important symbols of Easter. *(Answers on page 127.)*

Serve in Love

Kid Connection

Supplies: Bible Story Pak—p. 2, Stickers, sit-upons (see p. 14)

ASK: What animal is pictured in our New Life Connection this week? *(It's the monarch butterfly.)* How do you think a butterfly is a symbol of new life? *(Let the children contribute.)*

SAY: *(Refer to the illustration as you talk about the changes that occur in a butterfly that cause it to be a symbol of new life.)* The butterfly begins life as a teeny tiny little egg on the surface of a leaf. When the egg hatches, a small worm-like creature emerges. This larva begins to eat and eat and eat and eat. It becomes a caterpillar and continues to eat and eat and eat until the time is right. The caterpillar selects a perfect spot, attaches itself upside down to a branch, and

GROW • Proclaim • Serve • Middle Elementary Leader's Guide

spins a chrysalis. Inside that chrysalis, a marvelous change takes place. When the time is right, the chrysalis splits open, and a beautiful butterfly emerges.

SAY: As followers of Jesus, we want to reflect Jesus in our lives.

- Invite the children to place a butterfly sticker next to each word that shows the "new life" God is creating in each of us through Jesus.

- If you made the sit-upons and are adding a sticker for each story, add the final picture of the women at the empty tomb.

Make a Butterfly for the New Life Cross

Supplies: Reproducible 5b, large wooden craft sticks, 3-inch wire ribbon (a variety of colors), scissors, tape, glue sticks, white glue, rulers, crayons or markers

🕐 Photocopy the butterfly body and the directions for each child. If wire ribbon is not available, wide ribbon can be substituted.

SAY: The butterfly reminds us that as we learn more about what Jesus said and did, we become like new creatures, living and acting as Jesus taught.

- Have each child assemble a butterfly and bring it to worship. Remind the children to write their names on the backs so they can take them home after service.

Worship

Gather and Sing

Supplies: Bible Story Pak Songbooks, CD-ROM or DVD, CD player or DVD player, butterfly figures (see above), New Life Cross (see p. 11), tape

- Locate "A New Life" (Track #1) on the CD-ROM or DVD.

- Play the song and let the children sing it together.

SAY: Holy Week began in joy and ended in sadness. But the sadness did not last. When Mary Magdalene and the other Mary came to the garden, they found the tomb, but it was empty. God gave Jesus new life. And God promises that all those who believe Jesus is God's Son will have new life, too.

- The children will place their butterflies on the cross.

- Today is the last Sunday to add figures to the cross. You may choose to leave it up or take it down and give the children their crafts to take home after service.

Praise and Respond

Supplies: Bible, Bible Story Pak Songbooks, Reproducible 1c, Unit 1 Bible Story Poster Base and Pictures (see p. 12), CD-ROM, CD player, tape, Butterfly Shakers (see p. 32)

🕐 Locate the story picture for Session 5 (the empty tomb).

TIP

If the edges of the stickers are curling up or having difficulty sticking to the plastic, use clear masking tape to hold them down.

back

front

- Review the dance moves to "This Is the Day" (Track #5). Sing and move to the music. Invite the children to use their butterfly shakers.

SAY: Jesus is alive! God is more powerful than anything we can ever imagine. Even death is not as powerful as God. God raised Jesus from the dead. God gave Jesus new life. When we believe that Jesus is God's Son, God promises us new life, as well.

- Invite one of the children to read John 3:16.

- Then have one of the children place the picture from today's story on the poster with tape.

- Sing "This Is the Day."

- Invite the children to suggest any joys or concerns they would like to include in the closing prayer.

PRAY: Dear God, we thank you for Jesus, who came into the world to teach us how to live. We thank you for his life. We are thankful that you raised him from the dead. You are more powerful than we can imagine. Jesus is alive! Amen.

Plan for Next Week

Can You Find the Christians? (p. 52): Photocopy **Reproducible 6a** for each child. Cut a ½-inch hole in one side of each of the four shoeboxes, about 3 inches from the bottom edge of the box. Make sure there are no other light sources in the box. Make a copy of the picture cards, cut them apart, and tape one to the back wall of each shoebox (opposite of the hole).

Blindfold Scramble (p. 54): Photocopy **Reproducible 6b** at least four times. Cut the cards apart.

See the Light (p. 55): Photocopy **Reproducible 6c** for each child.

Reproducible 1a

1. Choose either a male or a female Bible character.
2. Color and cut out.
3. From a sheet of scrap paper, cut a strip of paper about 1-inch wide and 5-inches long.
4. Bring the two ends together to make a circle, and

secure with a piece of clear tape. Then use another piece of tape to attach the paper circle to the back of the puppet, about half an inch from the bottom. Only tape the side of the circle that's touching the puppet.
5. You should be able to put your index and middle fingers into the circle from above (with the back of your hand facing the puppet). Spread your fingers until the circle is tight, and then use them like legs to walk your puppet around.

Reproducible 1b

1. Cut out the frog body and legs.
2. Roll the body into a tube and glue, overlapping the edges slightly.
3. Glue the frog legs to the back of the body so that they stick out slightly on each side, as shown.
4. Add large wiggle eyes to the eye spaces so that they extend above the top edge of the body, as shown.
5. Add the frog to the New Life Cross using a loop of masking tape on the back.

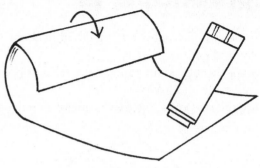

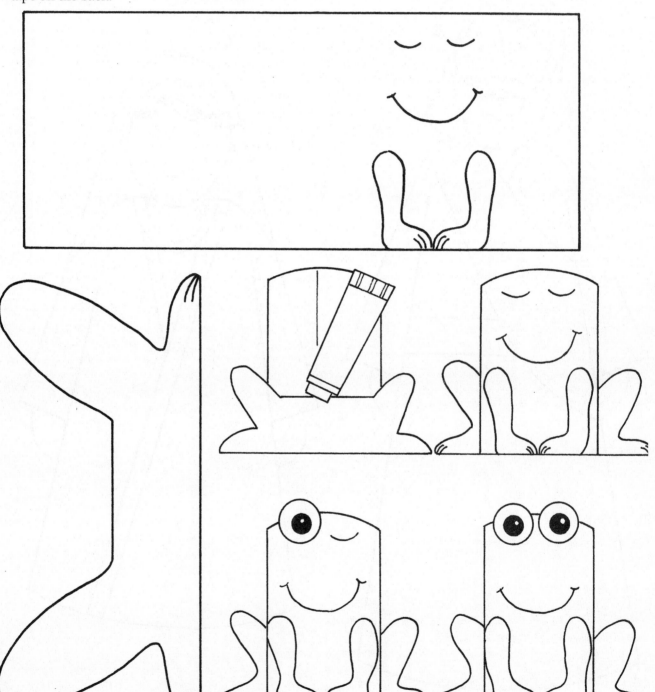

GROW • **Proclaim** • **Serve** • Middle Elementary Leader's Guide

Reproducible 1c

Let's Dance! (Movements for "This Is the Day")

Position 1: Begin with arms crossed in front of chest, right over left.

Position 2: Lift right arm in an arc until it is perpendicular to left arm.

Position 3: Extend right arm upward, making circles as it goes.

Position 4: Raise both hands overhead.

Position 5: Point to self and then point away from self.

Position 6: Take one step to the right and sweep right hand out to the right.

Position 7: Take one step to the left and sweep left hand out to the left.

Chorus:

(Begin in Position 1.)

This is the day (Position 2)

a miracle happened. (Position 3)

This is the day (Position 2)

our Savior came through. (Position 4)

This is the day (Position 2)

a miracle happened. (Position 3)

This is the day (Position 2)

for me and for you. (Position 5)

Verse:

Sing hallelujah, (Position 6)

Christ has risen. (Position 4)

Hallelujah, (Position 7)

oh, Wonderful One. (Position 4)

Sing hallelujah, (Position 6)

Christ has risen. (Position 4)

Hallelujah, (Position 7)

to God and to God's Son. (Position 4)

Reproducible 2a

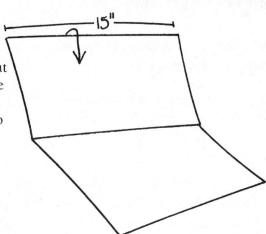

1. Fold a piece of table cover in half, forming a 15-inch square.
2. Use colored duct tape to seal two of the open edges. (**Hint:** Cut a piece of duct tape 15 inches long. Place along one of the side edges so that half the tape is on the table cover and the other half is on the table. Turn the sit-upon over and fold the tape to the other side. Repeat on the second edge.)
3. Fold newspaper sheets in half. Stack them on top of one another. Make several layers.
4. Slide the newspaper into the pocket of the table cover square. Then seal the remaining edge with another piece of duct tape.
5. All the boys and girls should sign one another's sit-upons.

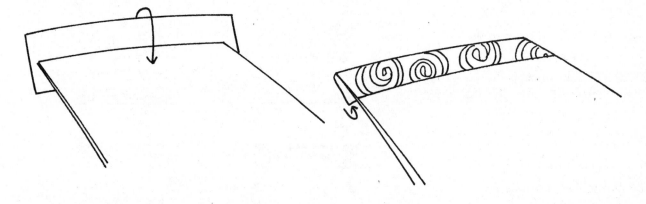

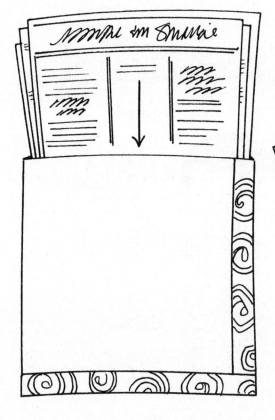

Add Stickers

Michael
Nicole
James
Stacie
Greg

GROW • **Proclaim** • **Serve** • Middle Elementary Leader's Guide

Reproducible 2b

1. Cut out the large egg and the "cracked" egg bottom. Decorate the pieces with crayons or markers, or trace them onto colored paper or art foam and cut out.
2. Put glue along the outside edge of the cracked egg bottom and glue it to the larger egg, forming a pocket.
3. Cut out the smaller egg shape. Trace onto yellow paper and cut out, or color the pattern yellow.
4. Add wiggle eyes to the smaller egg shape with white glue and feathers with tape, as shown.
5. Cut out the beak pattern. Trace it onto orange paper and cut out, or color it orange on both sides. Fold the beak in half along the dotted line, and glue the bottom triangle to the chick's face where indicated, so that the beak opens upward.
6. When the glue is set, insert the chick into the egg.

Reproducible 2c

People had so many eggs, they started to paint them and give them as gifts.

People had so many eggs, they started to paint them and give them as gifts.

for You—
Happy
Easter!

Long ago the church told people they could not eat eggs during Lent. But nobody told the chickens.

Today we fill beautiful baskets with the colorful eggs to remind us of the new life God promises to us.

The Story of the Easter Egg

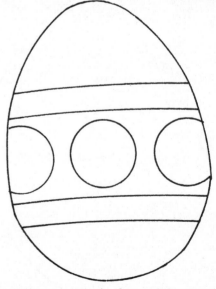

The egg is a symbol of new life. Inside the egg is a baby chicken ready to hatch.

GROW • **Proclaim** • **Serve** • Middle Elementary Leader's Guide

Reproducible 3a

1. Color and cut out the Pocket Puppets.
2. Fold on the dotted line.

3. Tape along the top and side, forming a pocket. Leave the bottom open.

4. Use the Pocket Puppets during the telling of the Bible story today.

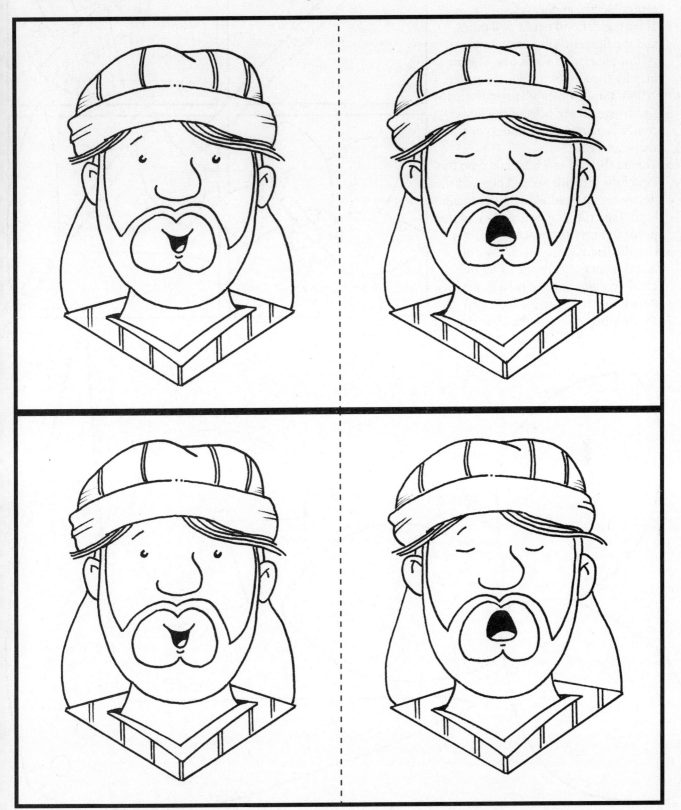

Reproducible 3b

1. Bend down the top inch of a green chenille stem, as shown.
2. Cut out the patterns for the daffodil center, petals, and leaves.
3. Trace the daffodil petals two times, and the flower center once, onto yellow paper. Cut them out. Or you may let the children color the patterns yellow. Punch holes where indicated.
4. Cut fringe on the edge of the flower center, as shown. Roll into a cone shape and glue.
5. Thread the two sets of petals onto the top of the chenille stem. Then add the flower center, leading with the smallest hole. Tape the stem to the back of the petals to keep it in place.
6. Use the leaf pattern to cut a set of leaves from green paper, or let the children color the leaf pattern green. Punch two holes where indicated.
7. Thread the bottom of the stem through the holes in the leaves, as shown.

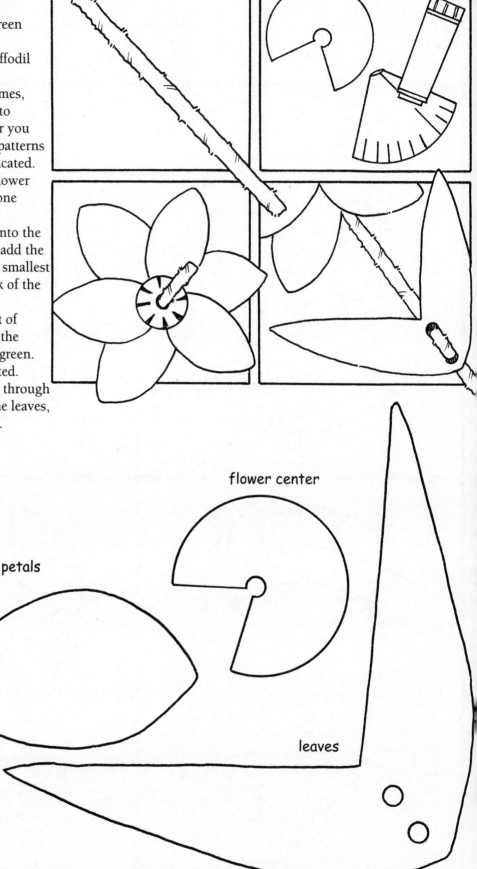

petals

flower center

leaves

GROW • **Proclaim** • **Serve** • Middle Elementary Leader's Guide

Reproducible 4a

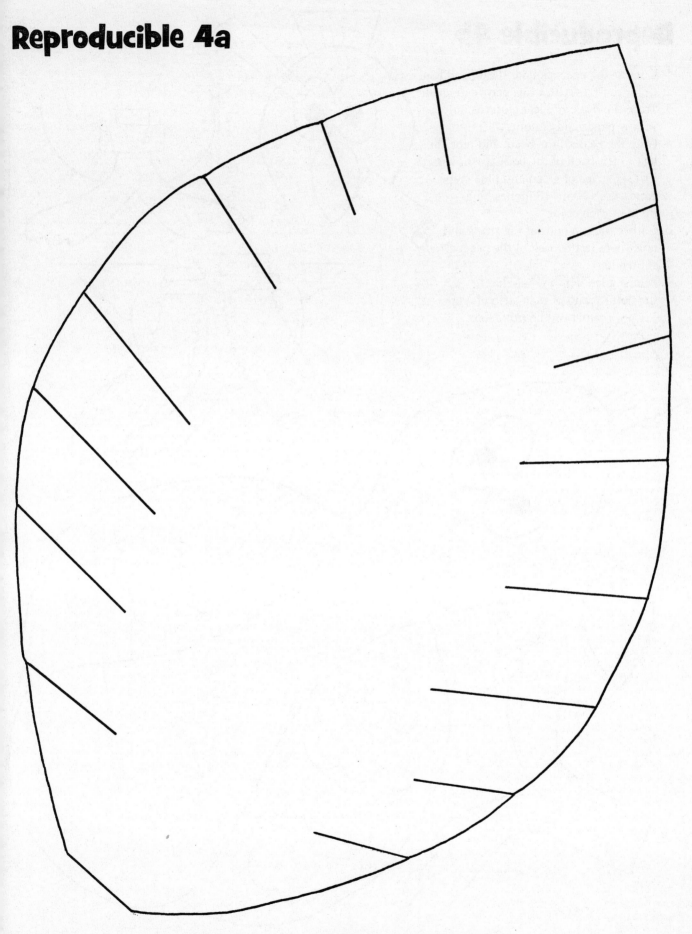

Reproducible 4b

1. Cut out the peacock body, beak, and feet.
2. Color the eyes with white crayon or chalk.
3. Trace the beak and feet patterns onto yellow paper and cut out.
4. Glue the beak to the head, and tape the feet to the back of the body, as shown.
5. Cut six strips of green and blue crepe paper, each about 18 inches long—three of each color.
6. Gather the top ends of the strips and tape them to the back of the peacock as shown here.
7. Attach a feather "eye" sticker to the bottom end of each strip of crepe paper on the front side.

Reproducible 5a

Reproducible 5b

1. Color and cut out the butterfly body and antennae. (Make sure you color both sides of the antennae.)
2. Fold the antennae in half at an angle (along the dotted line) so that they form a "V" as shown. Glue them to the back of the butterfly's head.
3. Glue the butterfly body to a large wooden craft stick (tongue depressor).
4. Cut two pieces of wide wire ribbon, each one 12 inches long.
5. Fold both ends of one piece of ribbon to the center and tape, as shown here. Do this with both pieces of ribbon.
6. Place the two ribbon loops side by side. Wrap a piece of tape around the center of both so that they look like wings, as shown.
7. Tape the "wings" to the back of the craft stick—the underside of the butterfly. (You may also want to add a little white glue.)

Antennae

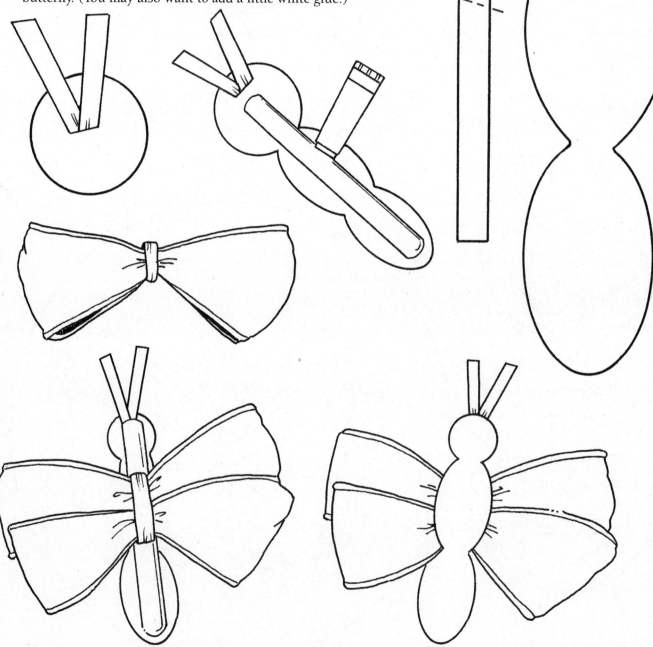

GROW • **Proclaim** • **Serve** • Middle Elementary Leader's Guide

Unit 2
A New Paul

Bible Verse

Believe in the Lord Jesus, and you will be saved. (Acts 16:31)

Leap of Faith

When I believe that Jesus is God's Son, my life changes.

In this unit

Session 6
April 7
Paul's Conversion
Bible story:
Acts 9:1-19

Session 7
April 14
Down the Wall
Bible story:
Acts 9:20-25

Session 8
April 21
Lydia
Bible story:
Acts 16:11-15

Session 9
April 28
Paul and Silas
Bible story:
Acts 16:16-40

CD-ROM

Changed (*Track #2*)
• vocal and instrumental
• lead sheet
• lyrics
• PowerPoint® lyrics

Growing in Leaps and Bounds (*Track #6*)
• vocal and instrumental
• lead sheet
• lyrics
• PowerPoint® lyrics

Leaper's Pointe (DVD)

Session 6
Paul's Conversion
Today's episode is about before and after. Papa B is admiring a vase that was broken into pieces—until Rosie gave it new life. Mrs. Finnanfeathers's caterpillar has become a butterfly, and Ernie's tadpoles have become frogs.

Session 7
Down the Wall
Ernie's pet frog, Saul, seems sad. Ernie goes to Mrs. Finnanfeathers for advice. Mrs. Finnanfeathers realizes that Ernie has been handling Saul so much that the other frogs think that Saul smells like people, not frog, and the other frogs are uncomfortable around him.

Session 8
Lydia
The mayor has given Ernie a riddle to solve. The clue is, "What do these words have in common—*Paul, God-fearer, Akhisar, shellfish,* and *merchant*?" They all have to do with the story of Lydia.

Session 9
Paul and Silas
Merrilee is reading a letter from a friend who's a missionary. This person and several of her friends just got out of jail. Their crime was passing out Bibles. The letter reminds the mayor of the Bible story about Paul and Silas in jail.

Leaper's Pointe in Concert (DVD)

• Changed
• Growing in Leaps and Bounds

Supplies

The Basics

CD player and/or DVD player
offering basket
scissors
markers (watercolor and permanent)
crayons
glue sticks

white glue
construction paper
colored copy paper
white copy paper
stapler, staples
paper punches
tape (clear, masking)
yarn/string
pencils

recycled newspaper
plastic drinking straws
lunch-sized paper bags
posterboard
rulers
plastic beads
chenille stems (a variety of colors)
wooden craft sticks

resealable plastic bags
wiggle eyes
ribbon (variety of widths)
cotton balls
cotton swabs
paper plates (variety of sizes and weights)

Beyond the Basics

Session 6
four shoeboxes or similar-sized boxes
blindfolds
6 clear plastic cups
liquid food coloring (red, blue, and yellow)
pitcher of water
toothpicks
black construction paper
dish towels or recycled newspaper
colored acetate paper (optional)
envelope

Session 7
unsharpened pencils or drinking straws
balloons
treats to give children
small box
faux gemstones or glitter (optional)
scraps of yarn (a variety of colors)

Session 8
purple yarn
magazine pictures of purple things
purple paper
purple fabric
large piece of blue fabric
purple crayons or markers
purple art foam
purple ribbon
purple felt-tip markers
magnetic strip tape

Session 9
black yarn
black construction paper
paper cups
dry cereal
moist towelettes
writing paper
keychain-sized ball chains or shower curtain rings

Tips

Session 6
If it's available, colored acetate paper can be used for both the "See the Light" poster and the "Seeing the Light" spectacles to make them extra fun.

Session 7
Try not to let the children put too many heavy items on their Crowns of Friendship. If it gets too heavy at the top, it will fall over and the "friends" won't stand up like they should.

Session 8
This session is all about the color purple, so make sure you have the correctly colored supplies before class on Sunday.

Session 9
You'll need two volunteers from the congregation to play Paul and Silas in the Bible story. You should make these arrangements beforehand to avoid any delays.

Reproducibles for Unit 2

These begin on page 75.

Paul's Conversion

Bible Verse
Believe in the Lord Jesus, and you will be saved. (Acts 16:31)

Bible Story
Acts 9:1-19

Leap of Faith
When I believe that Jesus is God's Son, my life changes.

Visit *GrowProclaimServe. com/leaders* to join the community with other leaders and find helpful weekly content and articles.

Before You Begin

Without the Book of Acts, we would know very little about the beginning of the early Christian church. Acts (the second half of the scroll known as Luke-Acts) gives us a glimpse into the lives of the men and women who carried the good news of Jesus to all the world. The writings in Luke-Acts tell us that the author was a person of deep faith and courage at a time when the new Christians feared for their lives. They were being persecuted from all sides. This scroll inspired those who read it to stand firm in their faith.

In today's story we meet Saul. (His Greek name was Paul. To avoid confusion with the children, we will be calling him Paul throughout, though you may want to mention that Saul and Paul are the same person.) His story and letters make up a large portion of the New Testament. Paul was a citizen of Tarsus, a metropolitan city of the Mediterranean. He came from a family of means and was obviously well-educated.

Paul started off his life as a righteous Jew, intending to put an end to this irritating group of men and women who followed Jesus. He was dedicated to stopping the spread of their subversive message, and he was willing to track them down wherever they might have taken refuge. He would find them and bring them back to Jerusalem for swift justice and imprisonment. And he was good at it. That was his reputation—until he met Jesus.

Children may be astounded to know that Paul was never one of the inner circle of twelve disciples. In fact, the disciples were quite afraid of him at first. So why is he so important? Paul became one of the single most influential missionaries of the Christian faith. Through Paul's conversion experience, the children can see that when Jesus comes into your life, your life literally changes and will never be the same again. In Paul's case, he was changed and rearranged.

Talking about "inside" changes may be a little difficult for seven- and eight-year-old children. These are more abstract ideas, and they are concrete thinkers. But if we put the message in terms of how we act and treat others, it will make an impression on them.

Requires preparation.

Grow Together

Choose one or more of the following activities to do as the children arrive.

Welcome the Children

Supplies: Resource Pak—pp. 2 & 23, Stickers, CD-ROM or DVD, CD player or DVD player, offering basket

- 🕐 Display the attendance chart from the Resource Pak.

- Play "Changed" (Track #2) and "Growing in Leaps and Bounds" (Track #6) as the children come into the room.

- Greet the children as they arrive.

- Show the children where to place their offerings.

- Give each child the attendance sticker for today to place on the chart.

Fun Pak Fun

Supplies: Fun Pak—p. 15, scissors, glue sticks, tape, colored acetate paper (optional)

- Have the children cut out and assemble the "Seeing the Light" spectacles. Let them choose three of the new life symbols to go on their new "shades." These symbols will remind the children of the stories they heard in the previous unit.

Just for Fun

Supplies: Bible Story Pak—p. 3, pencils

- The Bible Story Pak has four story and activity pages for each session. Remove the sheets for April 7. Give the children the Just for Fun page.

- Let the children follow the maze from Jerusalem to Damascus. (*Answer on page 127.*)

Can You Find the Christians?

Supplies: Reproducible 6a, scissors, four shoeboxes or boxes of a similar size, tape, pencils

- 🕐 Cut a ½-inch hole in one side of each of the shoeboxes, about three inches from the bottom edge of the box. Make sure there are no other light sources in the box. Make a copy of the picture cards, cut them apart, and tape one to the back wall of each shoebox (opposite of the hole). Photocopy a set of the picture cards for each child.

- Have the children cut out the pictures and write their names on the backs.

- Without picking up the boxes or removing the lids, have the children look through each hole and try to see which group of Christians is hiding inside. They will leave their own copies of the matching picture face-down beside the box.

- When everyone has decided which group of Christians is in each box, open the boxes and let the children see who guessed correctly.

ASK: Why was it so difficult to discover which picture was in each box? (*no light*)

TIP

Bible Factoids provide interesting tidbits of information about the Bible, Bible times, the land, or the culture. These will relate to the Bible story.

Conversation Time

Supplies: Birthday Celebration displays (see p. 8), crayons or markers, scissors, tape

🕐 Identify each child who has a birthday this week and make sure you have a birdhouse pattern and birthday gram for him or her.

- Bring the children together. They can sit around a table or on the floor. Give them a chance to briefly share any news of the week.

- Celebrate birthdays that have occurred or will occur in the coming week. Any child with a birthday can write his or her name on a birdhouse and color it. Add it to the birdhouse display on the wall, and give those children the birthday gram ("Tweet the news! _____ has a birthday.") to color and take home.

SAY: Can you imagine being a follower of Jesus after what happened in the garden? After everything you went through, you would be ready to tell everyone that Jesus is alive! But the same men who ordered that Jesus be put to death did their best to keep Jesus' followers quiet. *(Lower your voice to a whisper.)* If you met at all, you had to meet in secret. Some of the followers decided to leave Jerusalem. They ran away to nearby towns. *(Raise your voice back to normal.)* But that didn't help. The council actually sent people out to hunt them down and bring them back to Jerusalem for trial.

PRAY: Dear God, thank you for these boys and girls. We are proud to be followers of Jesus and to tell the good news about him to everyone, everywhere we go. We want to live as Jesus taught, always. Amen.

Proclaim the Word

Visit Leaper's Pointe

Supplies: DVD, DVD player

- The DVD is optional and can be used in place of "Interact With the Bible Story" or in addition to it.

- Place the DVD in the player. Locate Session 6.

- Invite the children to sit down where they can easily see the screen.

SAY: Today's episode is about "before and after." Papa B is admiring a vase that was broken into pieces—until Rosie gave it new life. Mrs. Finnanfeathers's caterpillar has become a butterfly, and Ernie's tadpoles have become frogs. These examples of new life are like Paul's story "before and after" he met Jesus.

- Watch the DVD segment.

Interact With the Bible Story

Supplies: Bible Story Pak—p. 1

SAY: In our earlier activity, we tried to find the Christians where they were hiding. But we couldn't because there was no light. Light makes a big difference—just ask Paul! When Paul saw the light, everything changed.

- Assign the parts and present the story from the Bible Story Pak.

All About the Story

ASK: Why was Paul going to Damascus? (*He had heard that some Christians were living there. He wanted to arrest them and bring them back to Jerusalem for trial.*) **What happened on the road?** (*He had a vision where Jesus appeared to him.*) **What did Jesus ask Paul?** (*Why are you harassing me?*) **After the vision went away, what did Paul discover?** (*He could no longer see.*) **What happened next?** (*Paul's fellow travelers led him into the city, where he waited until Ananias restored Paul's sight.*) **Then what did Paul do?** (*He told everyone the good news about Jesus.*)

SAY: Jesus had a plan for Paul, and it wasn't to arrest Christians. The vision that Paul had of Jesus that day changed his life forever.

Bible Connection

Supplies: Bible Story Pak—p. 4, pencils

- By filling in the names of things that give off light, the boys and girls will discover who Paul met on the road that day. Then they will fill in the missing letters of what this person asked Paul. (*Answers on page 126.*)

Blindfold Scramble

Supplies: Reproducible 6b, scissors, blindfolds

- ⏱ Photocopy the Bible verse cards at least four times. Cut them apart. Scatter them over a table top in random order.

- One at a time, have the children come to the table. Blindfold the child and have him or her choose four cards.

- Remove the blindfold. If the child can assemble the complete Bible verse using the cards he or she picked, the child gets a point.

- With a small class, the children can play multiple times.

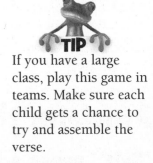

TIP

If you have a large class, play this game in teams. Make sure each child gets a chance to try and assemble the verse.

Serve in Love

Kid Connection

Supplies: Bible Story Pak—p. 2, Stickers, 6 clear plastic cups, food coloring (liquid, not gel, in red, blue, and yellow), pitcher of water

- Fill three of the cups with clear water and place them on a table so that the kids can see them.

ASK: What is in each cup? (*water*) **What color is it?** (*clear*)

- Add red food coloring to one cup, blue food coloring to another, and yellow to the third. Have the children identify each of the colors.

ASK: What will happen when I mix a little of the red with a little of the yellow in this cup? (*Have the children guess. Then pour about half the red water into an empty cup and add half the yellow. The water will turn orange.*) **What will happen**

GROW • **Proclaim** • **Serve** • Middle Elementary Leader's Guide

when I mix a little of the yellow with a little of the blue? (*Have the children guess, then pour half of each into one of the empty cups. The water will turn green.*)

- Repeat with the blue and the red to get purple.

SAY: Every time I mixed colors, they changed. But the liquid in each cup is still water. I didn't change anything but the color.

ASK: Who in today's story made a complete change? (*Paul*) Did he quit being "Paul"? (*No.*) How did he change? (*He acted differently.*)

SAY: Paul became a follower of Jesus, and he changed on the inside. He did things differently, even though he still looked the same on the outside.

- Have the children look at the different changes listed on the Bible Story Pak page.

SAY: Some of these changes are only outside changes. They are not changes that affect who we are. Some of these changes are inside changes that come about when we are followers of Jesus.

- Have the children mark the statements with either an "I" sticker for *inside* or an "O" sticker for *outside*. Then go over what choices they made and why.

See the Light

Supplies: Reproducible 6c, toothpicks, tape, black construction paper, dish towels or recycled newspaper, colored acetate paper (optional)

🕐 Photocopy the "Jesus Is the 1!" poster for each child.

- Have each child attach the poster to a piece of black construction paper using loops of tape on the back side. This keeps the poster from moving as the children are working on it.

- Place the poster and construction paper on newspaper or a dish towel.

- Have the children poke holes around the outline of the letters using their toothpicks.

Hint: Do not punch holes too close together or the paper will tear.

- Once the letters have been outlined, the children can add other decorative touches with their toothpicks by poking holes.

- When they have finished their decorations, have the children remove the "Jesus Is the 1!" posters from their pieces of construction paper.

TIP

For a cool option, glue colored acetate paper to the back of the poster after punching the holes.

SAY: When Paul met Jesus on the road to Damascus, he "saw the light." This meeting changed Paul's life forever. He became a new Paul—a Paul who was a follower of Jesus.

- Have the children hold their posters up to the light.

Worship

Gather and Sing

Supplies: Bible Story Pak Songbooks, CD-ROM or DVD, CD player or DVD player

- Locate "Changed" (Track #2) on the CD-ROM or DVD.
- Play the song through one time.

Believe

ASK: Who in today's story was changed? *(Paul)* How was he changed? *(He went from being someone who arrested Christians to being a Christian himself.)* How do you think this changed his life? His relationship with his friends? His relationship with the religious authorities back in Jerusalem?

- Hand out the songbooks.
- Practice spelling the word *changed* in rhythm.
- Sing the song together.

SAY: Today we begin hearing the stories about Paul and how his life changed after meeting Jesus. Believe me, it really changed!

Praise and Respond

Supplies: Bible, Bible Story Pak Songbooks, Resource Pak—pp. 9 (top) & 12-13, CD-ROM or DVD, CD player or DVD player, tape, envelope

Lord

🕐 Display the Unit 2 Bible Story Poster Base. Separate the pictures for Sessions 6-9. Locate the story picture for Session 6 *(Paul on the road to Damascus)*. Store the rest in an envelope for later sessions.

- Play the song "Growing in Leaps and Bounds" (Track #6) through one time. The children may be familiar with this song. Review the words if they are not.
- Sing the song together and move to the music.

SAY: On Easter Sunday we celebrated God giving Jesus new life. Today we celebrate the new life that Jesus gave to Paul. When we believe that Jesus is God's Son, God promises us new life, as well.

Jesus

- Invite one of the children to read Acts 16:31. Teach the children the signs for *believe*, *Lord*, and *Jesus* that are shown here. Read the verse again and let the children sign the first part.
- Then have one of the children place the picture from today's story on the poster with tape.
- Sing "Changed" (Track #2).

PRAY: Dear God, we thank you for Jesus, who came into the world to teach us how we should live. We thank you for Paul, whose life was changed when he met Jesus. Help us to live as Jesus taught in all we do each day. Amen.

Plan for Next Week

Kid Connection (p. 60): Draw a large gingerbread-type figure on a piece of recycled newspaper. (See illustration on page 60.)

Create a Crown of Friendship (p. 61): Photocopy the Crown of Friendship (**Reproducible 7b**) three times for each child. Photocopy the instructions (**Reproducible 7a**) once per child. You may also want to get some faux gemstones.

GROW • **Proclaim** • **Serve** • Middle Elementary Leader's Guide

Down the Wall

Bible Verse

Believe in the Lord Jesus, and you will be saved. (Acts 16:31)

Bible Story

Acts 9:20-25

Leap of Faith

When I believe that Jesus is God's Son, my life changes.

TIP

Visit *GrowProclaimServe. com/leaders* to join the community with other leaders and find helpful weekly content and articles.

Before You Begin

Paul had spent three days in total darkness, praying and fasting. By the time Ananias came to the house and touched him, he was already a changed man. Now he was filled with the passion of a man newly converted. He couldn't wait to share his experience with everyone.

Paul visited the synagogues in the area and proclaimed Jesus as God's Son. His enthusiasm, however, aroused the hostility of some of the Jewish religious authorities in the city. They made plans to silence Paul permanently. They posted guards along the gates, hoping to catch Paul as he left the city and kill him.

But God's purpose would not be denied. Paul's friends were prepared, and they planned a daring escape for him. The exterior walls of some of the houses in Damascus formed the perimeter wall of the city. Fellow believers took Paul to one of these houses and, in a large basket, lowered him from the outside window to the ground below. Once outside the city, Paul left for Arabia, where he preached for about three years.

Paul discovered right from the start that being a follower of Jesus was not going to be easy. First, he had to avoid people who, as he himself had been, were determined to arrest and imprison as many followers of Jesus as possible. Then he had to deal with his own reputation, since many of the other Christians still distrusted him. Paul discovered that being a Christian is more than an act—it is a way of life. With great enthusiasm he chose to be one of them, even knowing that there would be sacrifices along the way.

One of the things boys and girls need to know is that being a follower of Jesus does not mean that everything will always be fine. Sometimes there will be hard days and days when things don't come out as expected. Sometimes the things they pray for don't happen. Sometimes people get sick, people lose their jobs, and people even die. But as Jesus promised, God is always there with them. God will never leave them.

Requires preparation.

Grow Together

Choose one or more of the following activities to do as the children arrive.

Welcome the Children

Supplies: Resource Pak—pp. 2 & 23, Stickers, CD-ROM or DVD, CD player or DVD player, offering basket

🕐 Display the attendance chart from the Resource Pak.

- Play "Changed" (Track #2) and "Growing in Leaps and Bounds" (Track #6) as the children come into the room.

- Greet the children as they arrive.

- Show the children where to place their offerings.

- Give each child the attendance sticker for today to place on the chart.

Fun Pak Fun

Supplies: Bibles, Fun Pak—p. 17, scissors, glue sticks, yarn, rulers, paper punches

- Have the children cut out and assemble the Bible bookmark of Paul escaping down the wall in a basket.

- Locate the story for today (Acts 9:20-25) and place the bookmark there.

Just for Fun

Supplies: Bible Story Pak—p. 3, pencils

- The Bible Story Pak has four story and activity pages for each session. Remove the sheets for April 14. Give the children the Just for Fun page.

- The children will use the hidden letters to discover what Paul did in today's Bible story. *(Answer on page 126.)*

You Gotta Have Friends

Supplies: unsharpened pencils, balloons

- Divide the children into teams of two. Give each child an unsharpened pencil, and give each team an inflated balloon.

- Teams have to pick up the balloon using only their pencils and take it to a designated place on the other side of the room.

- If a balloon falls to the floor, team members have to work together to pick it up with their pencils and continue.

- The first team to get their balloon across the room wins the game.

ASK: Could you do this game with only one person? *(No.)*

SAY: Keep that in mind today as we hear more stories about Paul. He learned early that you've got to have friends.

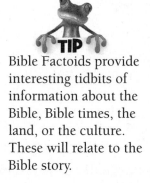

Bible Factoids provide interesting tidbits of information about the Bible, Bible times, the land, or the culture. These will relate to the Bible story.

If unsharpened pencils are not available, use plastic drinking straws.

Conversation Time

Supplies: Birthday Celebration displays (see p. 8), tape, scissors, crayons or markers, small box, treats

---

🕐 Identify each child who has a birthday this week and make sure you have a birdhouse pattern and birthday gram for him or her.

- Bring the children together. They can sit around a table or on the floor. Give them a chance to briefly share any news of the week.

- Celebrate birthdays that have occurred or will occur in the coming week. Any child with a birthday can write his or her name on a birdhouse and color it. Add it to the birdhouse display on the wall, and give those children the birthday gram ("Tweet the news! _____ has a birthday.") to color and take home.

- Place the small box about 10 feet away from you.

SAY: *(Name of one of the children)*, **I want you to bring me the box and I'll give you a treat.** *(More than likely, the child selected will pick it up and bring it to you.)* **Thank you.** *(Hand the child the treat and return the box to its original location.)* *(Name a different child)*, **I want you to bring me the box, but this time you can't touch it with your hands.**

- Continue using different criteria such as: You can't use your hands or your feet. You can't touch the box with any part of your body.

- When you have exhausted every possible way the children can move the box, have them sit down.

SAY: Well, it looks like the box just can't be moved. I can't think of a single way to move it that we haven't tried. That's what happens in today's Bible story. Paul needs to leave the city of Damascus. It isn't safe for him anymore. But all his normal routes of escape have been blocked. I wonder what he'll do.

PRAY: Dear God, thank you for these boys and girls. We are proud to be followers of Jesus and to tell the good news about him to everyone, everywhere we go. We thank you for Paul, who became a follower of Jesus. Amen.

Proclaim the Word

Visit Leaper's Pointe

Supplies: DVD, DVD player

- The DVD is optional and can be used in place of "Interact With the Bible Story" or in addition to it.

- Place the DVD in the player. Locate Session 7.

- Invite the children to sit down where they can easily see the screen.

SAY: Ernie's pet frog, Saul, seems sad. Ernie goes to Mrs. Finnanfeathers for advice. While Mrs. Finnanfeathers helps Ernie with his problem, Gabby tells the story of Paul in Damascus just after his conversion.

- Watch the DVD segment.

Interact With the Bible Story

Supplies: Bible Story Pak—p. 1

ASK: What have we learned from our games today?

SAY: We discovered that we couldn't do it alone and that we have to be creative in solving problems. In our Bible story, Paul discovers just how important each of these things is.

• Assign the parts and present the story from the Bible Story Pak.

All About the Story

ASK: Why was Paul having to leave Damascus? (*The religious leaders were angry with him. He had changed. He had become a follower of Jesus.*) **What did his friends suggest?** (*They suggested lowering Paul over the wall in a basket.*) **Does that sound dangerous?** (*Yes.*) **Why didn't Paul just go out the city gate?** (*The religious leaders had posted guards there to arrest him.*) **What do you think will happen next?**

SAY: Paul discovered that being a follower of Jesus wasn't going to be easy.

Bible Connection

Supplies: Bible Story Pak—p. 4, pencils

• Have the children fill in the blanks using the words on the sticky notes. (*Answers on page 126.*)

Knot Me!

• Have all the children stand in a circle with their hands extended.

• At the teacher's signal, each child will grab the hands of other children in the circle. They cannot grab the hand of the anyone directly to the right or left, and each hand must be joined to a separate person.

• Once everyone has grabbed hands, the children must untangle themselves without letting go of their companions' hands.

• The participants must communicate and work together to get untangled. Some of the players may end up facing outward, which is okay as long as no one lets go.

ASK: Do you think one person could have held the rope that lowered the basket? (*No.*) **What would have happened to Paul?** (*He would have been dropped.*)

SAY: Sometimes it takes all of us working together to do what God wants us to do.

TIP
This game is best played in a group of six to ten children.

Serve in Love

Kid Connection

Supplies: Bible Story Pak—p. 2, recycled newspaper, marker, pencils

🕐 Unfold a piece of recycled newspaper all the way and draw a body shape on it. It doesn't have to be perfect.

GROW • **Proclaim** • **Serve** • Middle Elementary Leader's Guide

ASK: Let's pretend that this person is the perfect friend. What would a perfect friend be like? (*As the children suggest words or phrases that describe a friend, write them inside the figure.*)

SAY: When Paul set off for Damascus, he wasn't trying to make friends—not at all. He wanted to arrest those troublesome Christians. But after he got there, this changed. He depended on the Christians there to help him escape from the city. Helping one another is just one of the things that Christians do.

- Have the children look at the picture in the Bible Story Pak and circle the boys and girls who are helping one another. Have them put an "X" over any kids who are not being helpful.

SAY: As followers of Jesus, we are called to be different, to care for others, to share, to (*use some of the phrases from the newspaper friend*).

Create a Crown of Friendship

Supplies: Reproducibles 7a & 7b, **Stickers**, scissors, tape, construction paper, crayons or markers, glue sticks, faux gemstones or glitter (optional), scraps of yarn

Try not to let the children put too many heavy items on their Crowns of Friendship. If it gets too heavy at the top, it will fall over and the "friends" won't stand up like they should.

🕐 Photocopy the Crown of Friendship pattern (**Reproducible 7b**) three times for each child. Photocopy the instructions (**Reproducible 7a**) once per child.

SAY: While Paul was in Damascus, he became like a new person. He went from being a hater of Christians to being a Christian himself. His life changed. The followers of Jesus in Damascus helped him escape. That's what followers of Jesus do—they help one another.

- Have the children create their crowns and wear them during worship.

Worship

Gather and Sing

Supplies: Bible Story Pak Songbooks, **CD-ROM or DVD**, CD player or DVD player

- Locate "Changed" (Track #2) on the CD-ROM or DVD.

- Play the song through one time.

ASK: Who is the person we've been learning about whose life changed? (*Paul*) How did he change? (*He went from being someone who arrested Christians to being a Christian himself.*) How do you think this changed his life? His relationship with his friends? What did his new friends do for him in today's story? (*They helped him escape from the city.*) Why did he need to escape? (*The religious authorities were planning to kill him.*)

- Hand out the songbooks.

- Practice spelling the word "Changed" in rhythm.

- Sing the song together.

SAY: Paul's life really changed. Something tells me it's going to change even more.

Praise and Respond

Supplies: Bible, Bible Story Pak Songbooks, Unit 2 Bible Story Poster Base and Pictures (see p. 56), **CD-ROM or DVD**, CD player or DVD player, tape

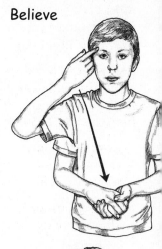

Believe

🕐 Locate the story picture for Session 7 *(Paul being lowered down the wall of the city at night)*.

- Play the song "Growing in Leaps and Bounds" (Track #6) through one time. The children may be familiar with this song. Review the words if they are not.

- Sing the song together and move to the music.

SAY: On Easter Sunday we celebrated God giving Jesus new life. Now we are talking about the new life that Paul had because he came to know Jesus. When we know that Jesus is God's Son, our lives change, too.

- Invite one of the children to read Acts 16:31. Review with the children the signs for *believe*, *Lord*, and *Jesus* that are shown here. Read the verse again and let the children sign the first part.

- Then have one of the children place the picture from today's story on the poster with tape.

- Sing "Changed" (Track #2).

Lord

PRAY: Dear God, we thank you for Paul, whose life was changed when he met Jesus. We thank you for the Christians in Damascus, who helped Paul and saved his life. We thank you for our friends and fellow Christians, who help us every day. Amen.

Plan for Next Week

Things I Know About Jesus (p. 64): Photocopy **Reproducibles 8a & 8b** for each child. Be sure you understand how to assemble the book so you can help the children put theirs together.

Jesus

Conversation Time (p. 65): You will need pieces of purple paper, strips of purple fabric, and pictures of purple items that have been cut out of magazines. Have these things already prepared before class on Sunday.

Sandals on a Mission (p. 67): Photocopy **Reproducible 8c** for each child. You will need purple art foam, purple ribbon, and magnetic strip tape for this activity.

Lydia

Bible Verse

Believe in the Lord Jesus, and you will be saved. (Acts 16:31)

Bible Story

Acts 16:11-15

Leap of Faith

When I believe that Jesus is God's Son, my life changes.

Before You Begin

During early New Testament times, in addition to the Jews, there were also Gentiles who believed in the one true God. These Gentiles observed the teachings of the Jewish faith and often even observed their special days. These Gentile believers were called "God-fearers." When Paul began his ministry to the Gentile communities, he made many converts to Christianity from among these Gentile believers.

A group of these God-fearers lived in Philippi, a city in Macedonia. As a Roman city, Philippi was not allowed to have a Jewish synagogue. So the God-fearers created their own alternative worship spaces. One of these meeting spaces was a riverbank outside the city walls. When Paul arrived in Philippi, he sought out one of the meeting places where a group of women came together to worship. He intended to bring the message of Jesus to them.

Lydia, a wealthy merchant, was a part of this group who met on the riverbank. Paul's message must have struck a note with her, because she and her whole family became believers. Lydia's conversion was significant because of her standing in the community. People took notice of anything she did. She opened many doors that might otherwise have been closed. Lydia offered Paul her home as a place to stay and continue his work. This sounds like a simple act of hospitality, but in the Roman world, facing the repercussions of such an act took great courage.

Paul was indeed living out his "new life." In the process of living this new life, he was bringing a new life to many other people, too. In this case, Lydia's life was also changed. The children may not realize how dangerous it was to be of a different faith in a Roman colony. It could mean persecution; it could also mean death. But these people were willing to put their faith ahead of any other considerations. Chances are, children today will not be persecuted for their belief in Jesus. But sometimes they may be called upon to stand against peer pressure, holding tight to their beliefs. Committing to follow Jesus means living according to Jesus' example—no matter the cost. What does this really mean to a seven- or eight-year-old? Loving God with all your heart, and loving your neighbor as yourself.

TIP

Visit *GrowProclaimServe.com/leaders* to join the community with other leaders and find helpful weekly content and articles.

Requires preparation.

Grow Together

Choose one or more of the following activities to do as the children arrive.

Welcome the Children

Supplies: Resource Pak—pp. 2 & 23, Stickers, CD-ROM or DVD, CD player or DVD player, offering basket

🕐 Display the attendance chart from the Resource Pak.

- Play "Changed" (Track #2) and "Growing in Leaps and Bounds" (Track #6) as the children come into the room.

- Greet the children as they arrive.

- Show the children where to place their offerings.

- Give each child the attendance sticker for today to place on the chart.

Fun Pak Fun

Supplies: Fun Pak—p. 19, scissors, glue sticks, purple yarn, rulers, paper punches

- Have the children cut out and assemble the purple belief banner. Remind the children that they can display their faith with pride.

Just for Fun

Supplies: Bible Story Pak—p. 3, pencils

- The Bible Story Pak has four story and activity pages for each session. Remove the sheets for April 21. Give the children the Just for Fun page.

- The children will draw a line between the puzzle piece pairs that go together. (*Answers on page 128.*)

Things I Know About Jesus

Supplies: Reproducibles 8a & 8b, Stickers, scissors, stapler

🕐 Make a copy of the "Things I Know About Jesus" book for each child.

SAY: We have been learning about a man named Paul. Paul became the greatest missionary the church has ever had. After a slightly shaky start, he began to travel around telling people all about Jesus wherever he went.

ASK: If you had been Paul, what are some things you would tell people about Jesus? (*Invite the children to share.*)

- Give each child the two "Things I Know About Jesus" sheets.

- Guide the children in cutting away the margins around the pages and folding the pages to make the book.

- Have the children add the pictures from the sticker sheet that match the statements about Jesus.

- Show the children how to place the second group of pages (with the dove

TIP

Bible Factoids provide interesting tidbits of information about the Bible, Bible times, the land, or the culture. These will relate to the Bible story.

GROW • Proclaim • Serve • Middle Elementary Leader's Guide

sticker facing up) inside the first group of pages (with the title sticker on the outside as the cover). Staple the pages together at the spine.

Conversation Time

Supplies: Birthday Celebration displays (see p. 8), tape, scissors, crayons or markers, purple paper and purple fabric cut into small pieces (about 1-2 inches), items that are purple from magazine pictures, posterboard, glue sticks

🕐 Identify each child who has a birthday this week and make sure you have a birdhouse pattern and birthday gram for him or her. Place purple magazine pictures, paper pieces, and cloth strips around the room.

• Give the children a chance to briefly share any news of the week.

• Celebrate birthdays that have occurred or will occur in the coming week. Any child with a birthday can write his or her name on a birdhouse and color it. Add it to the birdhouse display on the wall, and give those children the birthday gram ("Tweet the news! _____ has a birthday.") to color and take home.

SAY: Before we get started today, I want you to go on a "purple hunt." Around the room you will find pieces of purple fabric, purple paper, and purple pictures. See how many you can find and bring them to the conversation area, where we will glue them to a piece of posterboard.

• Give the children time to find the purple items and glue them to the posterboard.

• As they hunt, explain to the children that long ago the only way to create the color purple was to extract the dye from a shellfish. The shellfish could only be found in the Mediterranean Sea. It took a lot of these shellfish to make just a little dye, so purple dye was very expensive. Only the richest people could afford clothing that was dyed purple.

SAY: You found a lot of purple. Purple is one of my favorite colors. I'm sure it's also the favorite color of one of the people in our Bible story for today. Her name is Lydia, and her life changed because of Paul.

PRAY: Dear God, thank you for these boys and girls. We are proud to be followers of Jesus and to tell the good news about him to everyone, everywhere we go. We thank you for Paul, who became a follower of Jesus. We thank you that Paul was able to escape from Damascus to go on with his mission to spread the good news and change people's lives. Help us to follow his example. Amen.

Proclaim the Word

Visit Leaper's Pointe

Supplies: DVD, DVD player

• The DVD is optional and can be used in place of "Interact With the Bible Story" or in addition to it.

• Place the DVD in the player. Locate Session 8.

- Invite the children to sit down where they can easily see the screen.

SAY: The mayor has given Ernie a riddle to solve. The clue is "What do these words have in common—*Paul, God-fearer, Akhisar, shellfish,* and *merchant*?" Can you guess?

- Watch the DVD segment.

Interact With the Bible Story

Supplies: Bible Story Pak—p. 1, large piece of blue fabric

- Create a riverbank by spreading out a piece of blue fabric.

SAY: Paul was determined to tell the story of Jesus to anyone who could hear it. Today's story takes place on one of his journeys.

- Assign the parts and present the story from the Bible Story Pak.

All About the Story

ASK: Where was Paul in today's story? (*He was outside the city of Philippi on a riverbank.*) Why was he there? (*It was the Sabbath day, and they were looking for a place to worship God.*) Why didn't they just go to a church in the city? (*It was a Roman colony, and worshiping the one true God was forbidden.*) Who did Paul meet on the riverbank? (*He met some women who came there to worship.*) What did Paul tell them? (*He told them all about Jesus*) What happened next? (*Lydia became a follower of Jesus and invited Paul and Silas to stay in her home while they were in the city.*)

SAY: Everywhere Paul went, the story of Jesus went with him, and he shared it with everyone he met.

Bible Connection

Supplies: Bible Story Pak—p. 4, purple crayons or markers

- Have the children answer the question at the top of the page. Then they will mark out certain letters in the puzzle to discover what happened in today's story. (*Answers on page 128.*)

Touch Purple

Supplies: CD-ROM, CD player

- Have all the children stand up.

- Begin to play "Growing in Leaps and Bounds" (Track #6) from the CD-ROM.

- When you stop the music, everyone has to touch something purple.

- Anyone who is not touching purple by the time you count to three has to say something about the Bible story for today.

- Do this several times.

SAY: From now on, when you see purple, think of Lydia and her family.

TIP

Make sure there are at least a few purple things in the room before beginning the game.

Serve in Love

Kid Connection

Supplies: Bible Story Pak—p. 2, Stickers

SAY: Once Paul left Damascus safely, he wanted to tell the world about Jesus.

ASK: When he told Lydia about Jesus, what did she do? (*She became a follower of Jesus.*)

SAY: Paul was not shy about sharing his belief in Jesus with other people. If you were to find yourself in a strange country and somebody asked you, "Who is this Jesus?" what would you tell them? (*Let the children contribute.*)

- Have the children look at the statements on the Bible Story Pak page and put a smiling face sticker next to each thing about Jesus that is true. Put a frowning face sticker next to each statement that is not true. Just for fun, see if the children can "correct" the false statements.

Sandals on a Mission

Supplies: Reproducible 8c, purple art foam, paper punches, purple ribbon, rulers, scissors, masking tape, purple felt-tip markers, magnetic strip tape

🕐 Photocopy the sandal pattern for each child.

SAY: I'm glad I didn't have to buy sandals for Paul. He walked so many miles during his lifetime, I'm sure he wore out many pairs. Let's make a sandal out of purple materials to remind us of Lydia. We'll write the Bible verse on the sandal to remind us of Paul.

- Have the children follow the instructions to create their purple sandals.

SAY: When you see this sandal, it will remind you to share the good news about Jesus everywhere you go.

Worship

Gather and Sing

Supplies: Bible Story Pak Songbooks, CD-ROM or DVD, CD player or DVD player

- Locate "Changed" (Track #2) on the CD-ROM or DVD.

- Play the song through one time.

ASK: Who have we been learning about whose life was changed? (*Paul*) How did he change? (*He went from being someone who arrested Christians to being a Christian himself.*) How has this changed his life so far? (*Let the children share.*) Whose lives were changed today? (*Lydia and her family*) What caused them to change? (*Lydia became a follower of Jesus.*) Would that be a safe thing to do in the city where she lived? (*No, because it was against the law to worship the one true God in a Roman city.*)

- Hand out the songbooks.

- Sing the song together.

SAY: Paul's life has certainly changed. He changed Lydia's life, too. Something tells me more lives are going to change.

Praise and Respond

Supplies: Bible, Bible Story Pak Songbooks, Unit 2 Bible Story Poster Base and Pictures (see p. 56), **CD-ROM or DVD**, CD player or DVD player, tape

Believe

🕐 Locate the story picture for Session 8 (*Paul and Lydia with the other women on the riverbank*).

- Play the song "Growing in Leaps and Bounds" (Track #6) through one time. Review the words with the children. Then sing it together.

SAY: On Easter Sunday we celebrated God giving Jesus new life. Now we are talking about the new life that Paul had because he came to know Jesus. But Paul wasn't the only one with a new life. Everywhere he went, he took the story of Jesus with him. Everyone who heard it and believed began a new life, as well. And when we know that Jesus is God's Son, our lives change, too.

Lord

- Invite one of the children to read Acts 16:31. Review with the children the signs for *believe*, *Lord*, and *Jesus* that are shown here. Read the verse again and let the children sign the first part.

- Then have one of the children place the picture from today's story on the poster with tape.

- Sing "Changed" (Track #2).

PRAY: Dear God, we thank you for Paul, whose life was changed when he met Jesus. We thank you for the Christians in Damascus, who helped Paul and saved his life. We thank you for Lydia and her family, who heard the story of Jesus and believed. We thank you for these people who spread the good news so that we could hear the story of Jesus, too. Amen.

Jesus

Plan for Next Week

Make Manacles (p. 70): Cut black construction paper into 1½- by 8-inch strips. Each child will need eight strips.

Interact With the Bible Story (p. 71): Recruit two members of your congregation to play Paul and Silas in the drama from the **Bible Story Pak—p. 1.**

Keys That Unlock My Problems (p. 73): Photocopy **Reproducibles 9a & 9b** for each child. Each child will also need a keychain-sized ball chain or shower curtain ring.

Paul and Silas

Bible Verse

Believe in the Lord Jesus, and you will be saved. (Acts 16:31)

Bible Story

Acts 16:16-40

Leap of Faith

When I believe that Jesus is God's Son, my life changes.

Before You Begin

Paul and Silas were using Lydia's hospitality to continue their ministry in Philippi, a Roman city. During this time Rome had forcibly expelled all the Jews from the city of Rome. Citizens of other cities remained hostile toward the Jews who lived in their midst. Because many Christians were also Jews, the people did not distinguish between them. To them Christianity was merely a cult of the Jewish faith. In response, local communities established laws to keep the Jews from recruiting members into their religion. This was the setting in which Paul and his friend Silas were conducting their ministry.

When Paul exorcised the slave girl's demon in the public marketplace, he not only removed a lucrative source of income for her owners, he also broke the anti-propaganda law that was in place. He had the audacity to say, "In the name of Jesus Christ, I command you to leave her." From this moment on, the girl was no longer able to tell fortunes for her masters. What happened next was to be expected. Paul and Silas were arrested, beaten, and thrown into prison.

When the earthquake occurred and freed all the prisoners from their bonds, the jailer was convinced that he was a "dead man." He was certain that once freed, they would escape. How surprised he was to discover that all of them were still in their rightful places. The jailer then knew who he was dealing with. He took Paul and Silas to his own home, bandaged their wounds, and became a new believer. His life was completely changed.

Middle elementary boys and girls are just becoming aware of the world they have access to through television and the Internet. They probably don't realize what an open society the people of the United States of America enjoy. Here, people are allowed to practice their religions, whatever they might be, with no interference. It probably seems odd to them that someone would be arrested for simply healing someone in the name of Jesus. What the children are seeing in these stories is the Holy Spirit at work in the world. They see how God is with the faithful, even in the most dire circumstances. They see how even the most righteous of followers suffer for their faith.

TIP

Visit *GrowProclaimServe. com/leaders* to join the community with other leaders and find helpful weekly content and articles.

Requires preparation.

Grow Together

Choose one or more of the following activities to do as the children arrive.

Welcome the Children

Supplies: Resource Pak—pp. 2 & 23, Stickers, CD-ROM or DVD, CD player or DVD player, offering basket

🕐 Display the attendance chart from the Resource Pak.

- Play "Changed" (Track #2) and "Growing in Leaps and Bounds" (Track #6) as the children come into the room.

- Greet the children as they arrive.

- Show the children where to place their offerings.

- Give each child the attendance sticker for today to place on the chart.

Fun Pak Fun

Supplies: Fun Pak—p. 21, scissors, glue sticks, black yarn, rulers, paper punches, tape

- Have the children cut out and assemble Paul and Silas in their prison cell.

Just for Fun

Supplies: Bible Story Pak—p. 3, pencils

- The Bible Story Pak has four story and activity pages for each session. Remove the sheets for April 28. Give the children the Just for Fun page.

- Have the children follow the trail of chutes and ladders, writing the letters they find into the blanks at the top of the page in the correct order. *(Answer on page 126.)*

- As the children work, talk with them about all the adventures—some good and some not so good—that Paul has had as a missionary for Jesus.

Make Manacles

Supplies: black construction paper, scissors, rulers, tape or stapler

🕐 Cut black construction paper into 1½- by 8-inch strips. Each child will need eight strips.

- Have the children make a paper chain out of the black construction paper strips.

- Attach the first and last loops around their wrists to make manacles.

SAY: I am the jailer. I have heard that you are Christians. It is against the law to be a Christian in the city of Philippi. You are under arrest!

- Have the children come to the conversation area wearing their manacles.

TIP

Bible Factoids provide interesting tidbits of information about the Bible, Bible times, the land, or the culture. These will relate to the Bible story.

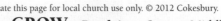

Conversation Time

Supplies: paper cups, dry cereal, Birthday Celebration displays (see p. 8), tape, scissors, crayons or markers

TIP
If there is a child with a birthday, make sure you celebrate it at some point. But keep in character for the moment.

- Have the children sit in silence on the floor with their legs extended. Give each "prisoner" a cup of dry cereal.

- Be sure to ask if there are any children with food allergies before handing out the cereal!

SAY: I have heard rumors that you are telling other people about this man Jesus. You are saying that he is the Son of the Most High God. This just cannot be. You are disobeying the laws. I think we should take you out and punish you. Troublemakers will not be tolerated here in Philippi.

- If a child tries to cross his or her legs or sit in any other way, stop them. (Unless there is a physical condition, this position will not cause any problems.)

SAY: You had better behave yourselves, too. According to Roman law, if anything happens to you, then I'm in big trouble. Over in the next cell are two men called Paul and Silas. All day long, all they do is sing and pray, sing and pray, sing and pray. It's beginning to get on my nerves.

Proclaim the Word

Visit Leaper's Pointe

Supplies: **DVD,** DVD player

- The DVD is optional and can be used in place of "Interact With the Bible Story" or in addition to it.

- Place the DVD in the player. Locate Session 9.

- Invite the children to sit down where they can easily see the screen.

SAY: Merrilee is reading a letter from a friend who's a missionary. She and several of her friends just got out of jail. Their crime was passing out Bibles. The letter reminds the mayor of the Bible story about when Paul and Silas were thrown into jail for telling others about Jesus.

- Watch the DVD segment.

Interact With the Bible Story

Supplies: Bible Story Pak—p. 1, moist towelettes

- 🕐 Invite two congregation members to play the parts of Paul and Silas. You continue to be the jailer.

- Make sure the children are still manacled, and continue with the drama.

SAY: I'm bringing Paul and Silas in here with you. It will be easier to keep an eye on all of you.

- Present the story from the Bible Story Pak.

- When you come to the earthquake, have the children remove their manacles. Afterwards, wipe the children's hands with the moist towelettes.

SAY: I'm so sorry for all the indignities you have received. Go in peace.

All About the Story

ASK: Where was Paul in today's story? *(Philippi, in jail)* Why was he there? *(He had driven a spirit out of a slave girl so she could no longer tell fortunes.)* Why was this a problem? *(Her masters depended on the income she earned.)* What happened next? *(Paul and Silas were beaten and thrown into prison.)* What happened next? *(An earthquake freed the prisoners.)* What happened next? *(The jailer discovered that the prisoners were not gone and that Paul and Silas were special people.)* Whose life was changed in today's story? *(the jailer, who became a follower of Jesus)*

SAY: Everywhere Paul went, the story of Jesus went with him and he shared it—even in prison.

Bible Connection

Supplies: Bible Story Pak—p. 4, pencils

- Have the children finish the puzzle by writing in the missing letters to discover what Paul and Silas did everywhere they went, no matter what. *(Answer on page 128.)*

Songs of Comfort and Joy

Supplies: writing paper, pencils

- Divide the children into pairs.

- Assign each pair a familiar tune such as "Twinkle, Twinkle, Little Star" or "Mary Had a Little Lamb."

ASK: What songs did Paul and Silas sing while they were in that prison cell?

SAY: We don't know. But it was probably unusual for prisoners to sing. Often people sing or listen to music when they are feeling down or sad or unhappy. Let's create some songs we can sing when we need perking up.

- Give the children time to create their own songs. They will make up their own words and sing them to a familiar tune. We call these "piggy-back songs."

- Let them share the songs with the group.

TIP

If you have a large group, divide them into groups of four. If you have only two or three children, let them all work together.

Serve in Love

Kid Connection

Supplies: Bible Story Pak—p. 2

SAY: Paul shared the good news about Jesus no matter where he was. He shared it in a strange city; he shared it on a riverbank; he even shared it while he was in jail.

- Have the children take turns reading aloud the short paragraphs from the Bible Story Pak.

- Then ask the boys and girls who in each little story is sharing the good news and how it is different than what someone might expect.

Keys That Unlock My Problems

Supplies: Reproducibles 9a & 9b, scissors, glue sticks, keychain-sized ball chains or shower curtain rings, paper punches

🕐 Photocopy the locks and keys for each child. Each child will need a set of both pages.

ASK: *(After each question, you might want to let some of the children share if they feel inclined to do so.)* Can you think of a time when you were afraid? Anxious? Depressed? Have you ever been disappointed or discouraged? Have you ever felt harassed by other kids? Or hopeless? Have you ever felt so tired that you didn't know what to do?

SAY: We all have problems now and then. Even Paul had problems. He was afraid on the road to Damascus. He was anxious as he was lowered down the wall in a basket. He was discouraged when he found himself in prison. But God was there with him, and he learned to persevere in spite of his problems.

- Give each child a set of the locks and keys. Identify the different problems that are printed on the locks.

SAY: There are solutions to our problems. All we have to do is look in the Bible. The Bible provides answers for us.

- Have the children cut out each lock/key pair along the solid lines. Fold each pair on the dotted line, and glue both sides together. When dry, punch a hole at the X and thread all the pairs onto a keychain.

SAY: Attach this to your backpack or carry it in your pocket or purse. When you have one of these problems, just read what the Bible says about it. Ask God to help you.

Worship

Gather and Sing

Supplies: Bible Story Pak Songbooks, CD-ROM or DVD, CD player or DVD player

- Locate "Changed" (Track #2) on the CD-ROM or DVD.

- Play the song through one time.

ASK: Who have we been learning about whose life was changed? *(Paul)* How did he change? *(He went from being someone who arrested Christians to being a Christian himself.)* How has this changed his life so far? *(Let the children share.)* Whose lives were changed today? *(the jailer and his family)* What caused them to change? *(When the earthquake set the prisoners free, Paul and Silas did not leave.)* What did he do then? *(He brought them to his home, cared for their injuries, and became a follower of Jesus.)*

- Hand out the songbooks.

- Sing the song together.

SAY: Paul's life has certainly changed. He changed Lydia's life, and he changed the jailer's life, too. Wherever Paul went, he changed the lives of the people who heard his good news message.

Praise and Respond

Supplies: **Bible, Bible Story Pak Songbooks, Unit 2 Bible Story Poster Base and Pictures** (see p. 56), **CD-ROM or DVD,** CD player or DVD player, tape

Believe

🕐 Locate the story picture for Session 9 (*Paul and Silas in prison*).

- Play the song "Growing in Leaps and Bounds" (Track #6) through one time. The children may be familiar with this song. Review the words if they are not.

SAY: On Easter Sunday we celebrated God giving Jesus new life. We have learned about the new life that Paul was living because he came to know **Jesus.** (*Review the stories on the poster about Paul, using the pictures.*) **Everyone who heard Paul's message and became a believer began a new life. When we know that Jesus is God's Son, our lives change, too.**

- Invite one of the children to read Acts 16:31. Review with the children the signs for *believe, Lord,* and *Jesus* that are shown here. Read the verse again and let the children sign the first part.

Lord

- Then have one of the children place the picture from today's story on the poster.

- Sing "Changed" (Track #2).

PRAY: Dear God, we thank you for Paul, whose life was changed when he met Jesus. We thank you for the Christians in Damascus, who helped Paul and saved his life. We thank you for Lydia and her family, who heard the story and believed. We thank you for the jailer and his family, who cared for Paul and Silas. We thank you for these people, who believed the good news and spread it to others. Amen.

Jesus

Plan for Next Week

Make "Keepers of the Flame" Torches (p. 88): Photocopy **Reproducible 10a** for each child.

Cooperative Bible Verses (p. 90): Photocopy **Reproducible 10b** once for every six children. There are two sets of Bible verse words and two sets of clues on the page. Cut them apart along the solid lines and put each set of clues in an envelope. Then paper clip the matching set of Bible verse words to the outside of each envelope.

Make Good Neighbor Boxes (p. 91): Photocopy **Reproducibles 10c & 10d** for each child. You may want to use colored paper for photocopying **Reproducible 10d.**

Next week is the beginning of this quarter's mission project. You should become familiar with the information on **Reproducible 10c** and **Bible Story Pak—p. 2.** Prepare a collection container for this project and make any arrangements necessary for donating the money at the end of the month.

Reproducible 6a

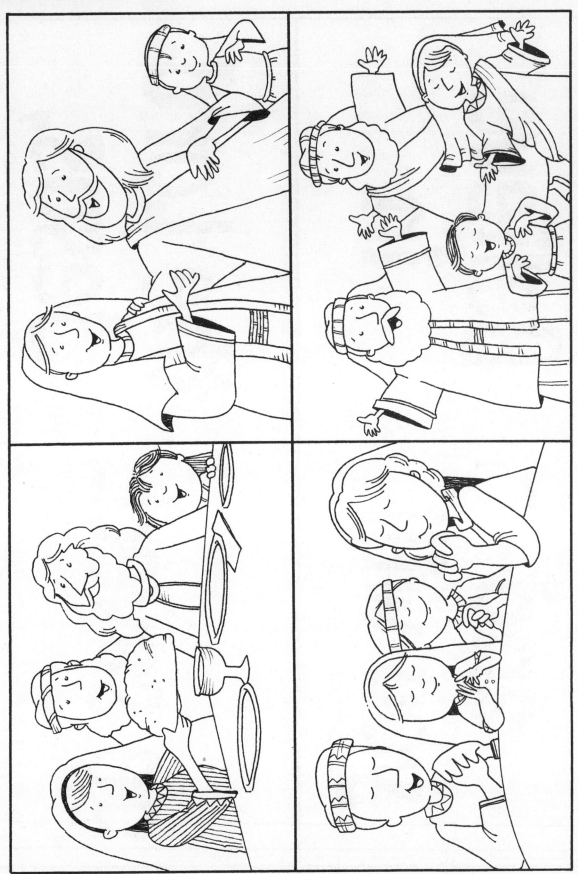

Believe in

the Lord Jesus,

and you will

be saved.

Reproducible 7a

1. Start with three copies of the crown segment. Cut them out and tape them end to end. You will probably only need 2½ segments.
2. Fit the crown to your head and cut off the extra length, leaving just enough to have a 1- or 2- inch overlap. Wait to tape the crown together until after you decorate.
3. Draw and cut hair from construction paper or yarn scraps. Look at the illustrations here for ideas.
4. Glue the hair onto each person on the crown.
5. Draw a face and clothes on each person. Be imaginative and think of some interesting facial expressions to give them more character.
6. Attach the friendship word stickers to your crown.
7. Wrap the crown around your head and have a friend help tape it together.

Cool Option: Add faux gemstones or glitter to your crown to give it a little "bling."

Add Stickers

GROW • **Proclaim** • **Serve** • Middle Elementary Leader's Guide

Reproducible 7b

Reproducible 8a

fold this side down first

Jesus was put to death on a cross.

Jesus was born in a stable.

Add
Cross
Sticker

Add
Star
Sticker

fold this side across second

Add
Butterfly
Sticker

Add
Things I Know About Jesus
Sticker

God raised Jesus from the dead.

Reproducible 8b

fold this side down first

Jesus told people how to live.

Jesus called fishermen to be his helpers.

Add
Bible
Sticker

Add
Fishing
Sticker

Add
Hands
Sticker

Add
Dove
Sticker

Jesus healed the sick.

Jesus was baptized by John.

Reproducible 8c

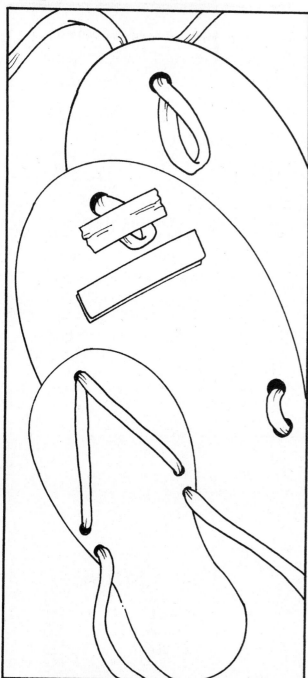

1. Use the pattern to cut a sandal base out of purple art foam.
2. Punch holes where indicated.
3. Cut an 18-inch length of purple ribbon.
4. Fold the ribbon in half and thread about an inch of the folded end through the top hole in the sandal.
5. Tape the folded end to the back side of the sandal with masking tape as shown.
6. Attach a 2-inch strip of magnetic tape on the back side of the sandal, under the taped end of the ribbon.

7. Separate the two loose ends of the ribbon. Thread one through the two holes on the left side of the sandal, and the other through the holes on the right, as shown. Tie into a bow.
8. With a purple felt-tip marker, write the Bible verse on the sandal (Acts 16:31).

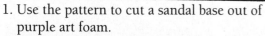

GROW • **Proclaim** • **Serve** • Middle Elementary Leader's Guide

Reproducible 9a

The LORD is for me—
I won't be afraid.
Psalm 118:6

Cast your burden on the
LORD—he will support you!
Psalm 55:22

Glory to God, who is able
to do far beyond all that
we could ask or imagine by
his power at work within us.
Ephesians 3:20

X

X

X

I feel afraid

I feel anxious

I feel disappointed

Reproducible 9b

But the LORD is the one who is marching before you! He is the one who will be with you! He won't let you down.
Deuteronomy 31:8

Anyone who wants to live a holy life in Christ Jesus will be harassed.
2 Timothy 3:12

Be happy in your hope, stand your ground when you're in trouble, and devote yourselves to prayer.
Romans 12:12

X

I feel discouraged

X

I feel harassed

X

I feel hopeless

GROW • **Proclaim** • **Serve** • Middle Elementary Leader's Guide

Unit 3
New Believers

Bible Verse

The community of believers was one in heart and mind. (Acts 4:32)

Leap of Faith

As a Christian, I am called to care for others.

In this unit

Session 10
May 5
The Community of Believers
Bible story:
Acts 2:42-47; 4:32-35

Session 11
May 12
Peter and Cornelius
Bible story:
Acts 10:1-28

Session 12
May 19
Pentecost
Bible story:
Acts 2:1-41

Session 13
May 26
First Called Christians
Bible story:
Acts 11:19-26

CD-ROM

True Believers (*Track #3*)
- vocal and instrumental
- lead sheet
- lyrics
- PowerPoint® lyrics

Keep the Faith (*Track #4*)
- vocal and instrumental
- lead sheet
- lyrics
- PowerPoint® lyrics

Leaper's Pointe (DVD)

Session 10
The Community of Believers
The townspeople are finishing up a yard sale to help Mr. Campbell with his medical bills. Next is a community dinner where everyone has contributed something. They are like the early Christians who were one in heart and mind.

Session 11
Peter and Cornelius
Harley is upset. Coach Mondo won't let him play on the town baseball team because Harley is left-handed. Merrilee tells the story of Peter baptizing the Gentile Cornelius as a follower of Jesus. Mondo finally has a change of heart, and everyone is welcomed on the team.

Session 12
Pentecost
It's "Celebrate-the-Wind Day" in Leaper's Pointe, and things are really blowing around! There are bubbles, banners, balloons, kites, pinwheels, wind chimes, streamers, and flags. Merrilee explains that this is not only the time that Leaper's Pointe celebrates the wind, it's also the time that Christians celebrate Pentecost.

Session 13
First Called Christians
Merrilee is counting the suggestions for what to name the citizens of Leaper's Pointe. Mondo is sure his suggestion will win, but Merrilee is not so sure. She remembers the trouble her Nana had trying to find a name for the townspeople. Like Nana, Merrilee thinks names are nice, but that what's inside matters more.

Leaper's Pointe in Concert (DVD)

- True Believers

Supplies

The Basics

CD player and/or DVD player
offering basket
scissors
markers (watercolor and permanent)
crayons
glue sticks

white glue
construction paper
colored copy paper
white copy paper
stapler, staples
paper punch
tape (clear, masking)
yarn/string
pencils

recycled newspaper
plastic drinking straws
lunch-sized paper bags
posterboard
rulers
plastic beads
chenille stems (a variety of colors)
wooden craft sticks

resealable plastic bags
wiggle eyes
ribbon (variety of widths)
cotton balls
cotton swabs
paper plates (variety of sizes and weights)

Beyond the Basics

Session 10
art tissue (red, orange, yellow)
envelopes
paper clips
world map or globe

Session 11
mission project collection container
solid colored paper or fabric
2 plastic forks
1 plastic spoon
world map or globe
old magazines
red copy paper
paper fasteners
black poster paint
shallow lids
hand-cleaning supplies
black markers

Session 12
mission project collection container
red paper
ball-head straight pin
unsharpened pencil
index cards
red crepe paper
world map or globe
paper cutter
art tissue (red, orange, and yellow)
old file folders or cardstock

Session 13
mission project collection container
colored duct tape
dishpan or baking pan
sand
stick
world map or globe

Tips

Session 10
This week is the beginning of this quarter's mission project. You should become familiar with the information on **Reproducible 10c and Bible Story Pak—p. 2.**

Session 11
Be sure you've got some hand-cleaning supplies before you start making the Mother's Day ladybugs. The children will be using poster paint, and it could get messy!

Session 12
Add a small paper clip to the bottom of any flaming wind walker (from the Fun Pak) that "flops" more than it "walks."

Session 13
This is the last Sunday to collect money for the Kamina Project. Send what you've collected to the address on page 110.

Reproducibles for Unit 3

These begin on page 111.

The Community of Believers

Bible Verse

The community of believers was one in heart and mind. (Acts 4:32)

Bible Story

Acts 2:42-47; 4:32-35

Leap of Faith

As a Christian, I am called to care for others.

Before You Begin

The Book of Acts is the second part of the scroll known as Luke-Acts, which was written by the same person. This scroll tells us much about what life was like among the early followers of Jesus. Now that they were on their own, the new faith community centered on a common life together. They spent their time teaching, worshiping, serving, and praying. This common life gave them a vision of what Jesus meant when he talked about the "kingdom of God." Throughout Luke-Acts, the writer emphasizes that Jesus himself directed this new Christian movement.

At first the followers of Jesus were just one among many Jewish sects. They continued to be Jewish at first and maintained the rituals, traditions, and identity of their faith. They did believe, however, that Jesus was the fulfillment of the prophecies from the Hebrew Scriptures and that he would be returning at any time, bringing the long-awaited kingdom of God with him. The people were filled with an urgent need to share the good news with everyone they could as quickly as they could. A close community with mutual support and combined resources made this a reality. Later, when the Christians broke their ties to the Jewish faith, conflict ensued and many believers left Jerusalem. But wherever they went, they took their faith with them and started new churches. The good news of Jesus began to spread exponentially.

Middle elementary boys and girls are a part of the church. If they are made to feel from an early age that they are contributing members of the faith community, then they will not choose to leave it as they get older. "Belonging" carries with it a feeling of letting others down when you are not there to participate. You can create this sense of belonging by including intentional group-building activities during the Conversation Time. Pray for one another. Encourage the children to be mutually supportive, caring, and in touch with one another as part of what it means to be a disciple of Jesus.

TIP

Visit *GrowProclaimServe. com/leaders* to join the community with other leaders and find helpful weekly content and articles.

Requires preparation.

Grow Together

Choose one or more of the following activities to do as the children arrive.

Welcome the Children

Supplies: Resource Pak—pp. 2 & 23, Stickers, CD-ROM, CD player, offering basket

🕐 Display the attendance chart from the Resource Pak.

- Play "True Believers" (Track #3) and "Keep the Faith" (Track #4) as the children come into the room.

- Greet the children as they arrive.

- Show the children where to place their offerings.

- Give each child the attendance sticker for today to place on the chart.

Fun Pak Fun

Supplies: Fun Pak—p. 23, scissors, glue sticks

- Have the children cut out and assemble the color wheel and base.

- Have them blow on the wheel and watch what happens to all the colors.

Just for Fun

Supplies: Bible Story Pak—p. 3, pencils

- Remove the sheets for May 5 from the Bible Story Pak. Give the children the Just for Fun page.

- The children will write the first letter of the name of each picture in the space provided. When completed, it will spell out the answer to the question, "What was so special about the followers of Jesus?" *(Answers on page 126.)*

Make "Keepers of the Flame" Torches

Supplies: Reproducible 10a, crayons or markers, art tissue (red, orange, and/or yellow), tape, scissors

🕐 Photocopy the torch base for each child.

- Have the children color and cut out the torch base, roll it into a cone shape, and tape it in place.

- Fold a sheet of colored art tissue in half. Then fold it in half the opposite way with the folded edges together.

- Repeat folding in this direction until the sheet is about five inches wide.

- With a pair of scissors, cut toward the folded edge, stopping about two or three inches from the edge. Do this several times to make fringe.

- Unfold the art tissue. Gather the edge that's not cut and tape, as shown.

- Stuff the fringed tissue bundle into the torch, deep enough that it doesn't flop out.

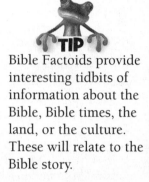

• Have the children bring their torches to the conversation area.

Conversation Time

Supplies: Birthday Celebration displays (see p. 8), tape, scissors, crayons or markers, "Keepers of the Flame" Torches (see p. 88)

TIP

Have the children write their names on their torches so they can take them home at the end of the Session 11.

• Have the children sit either in chairs or on the floor.

• Celebrate any birthdays that have occurred or will occur in the coming week. Use the birdhouse patterns and birthday grams.

ASK: *(Hold up one of the torches.)* **What do you use a torch for?** *(to provide light)* **What provides the light?** *(a flame)* **Can you think of a time when you might use a torch?** *(Invite the children to share their ideas.)*

SAY: Today we are going to begin a new unit. It's called "New Believers." We are going to hear stories of what happened to the first followers of Jesus after Jesus left to be with God. We will learn how it came to be that the stories of Jesus spread and spread so that we know the stories today and read them in our Bibles. We will also see how it is now our job to keep spreading the good news of Jesus. We will be like the Olympic flame this past summer, carrying on the faith without letting it burn out.

Proclaim the Word

Visit Leaper's Pointe

Supplies: DVD, DVD player

• The DVD is optional and can be used in place of "Interact With the Bible Story" or in addition to it.

• Place the DVD in the player. Locate Session 10.

• Invite the children to sit down where they can easily see the screen.

SAY: The townspeople are finishing up a yard sale to help Mr. Campbell with his medical bills. Next is a community dinner where everyone has contributed something. They are like the early Christians who were one in heart and mind.

• Watch the DVD segment.

Interact With the Bible Story

Supplies: Bible Story Pak—p. 1, "Keepers of the Flame" Torches (see p. 88)

• Have the children sit in a circle.

SAY: It's good to help one another. That's what Jesus taught while he was here on earth. That's what the Bible tells us, too. As we present the drama, every time you hear the word "Jesus," I want you to pass your torch to the right.

• Assign the parts and present the story from the Bible Story Pak, passing the torches every time the word "Jesus" comes up in the drama. Then have the children save their torches to bring to the worship area.

All About the Story

SAY: Jesus was no longer on the earth. But Jesus' teachings still lived among the followers. Every time they met together and shared with one another, they were keeping the words of Jesus alive.

ASK: Why do you think the people were anxious to talk to Andrew? *(He had actually known Jesus, talked with him, and traveled with him.)* **Why was this important?** *(Most of these people had only heard stories about Jesus. They wanted to know what was really true.)* **What did Barnabas do that showed he was a true follower of Jesus?** *(He sold a field and gave the money to the apostles to use.)*

SAY: At this point, most of Jesus' followers still lived in and around Jerusalem. But that was soon to change. The good news of Jesus was on the move. Paul helped it to spread, and other followers would do the same.

Bible Connection

Supplies: Bible Story Pak—p. 4, pencils

- Have the children use the code to discover what members of the early church did, and then draw lines to connect the statements with the matching pictures. *(Answers on page 126.)*

Cooperative Bible Verses

Supplies: Reproducible 10b, scissors, envelopes, paper clips

🕐 Make one copy of the reproducible page for every six children. There are two sets of Bible verse words and two sets of clues on the page. Cut them apart along the solid lines and put each set of clues in an envelope. Then paper clip the matching set of Bible verse words to the outside of each envelope.

- Divide the children into teams of three.

- Give each team one envelope with the Bible verse words paper clipped to the outside. Have them pass out the clues from inside the envelope to their team. (There are seven clues, so one person will get three clues instead of two.)

- Have the children spread out the Bible verse words on the table. They will take turns reading their clues until they've put the Bible verse into the correct order.

SAY: You couldn't have done it without your team. Jesus' followers worked together, too. They supported one another. This was important, because their neighbors who were not followers of Jesus didn't like them very much.

> **TIP**
> If you have a small group, let all the boys and girls be part of one team. When they finish one Bible verse, let them work cooperatively on the second.

Serve in Love

Kid Connection

Supplies: Bible Story Pak—p. 2, world map or globe

ASK: Who is our neighbor? Is *(name one of the children)* our neighbor? Is *(name the pastor of your church)* our neighbor? Is your teacher at school your neighbor?

SAY: Our neighbor is anyone who needs our help. Some of our neighbors are the boys and girls who live in Kamina, a town in the Democratic Republic of the Congo. *(Point to the country on the globe or world map.)* Even though these boys and girls live on the other side of the globe, they are our neighbors, and they need our help.

- Invite the children to read in the Bible Stork Pak about the mission project for this quarter.

SAY: The money that we collect in the next three weeks will go toward helping the people of Kamina have clean water, good food, a good education, and all the little things we take for granted.

Make Good Neighbor Boxes

Supplies: Reproducibles 10c & 10d, Stickers, scissors, tape, colored copy paper (optional)

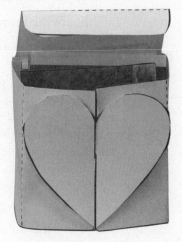

🕐 For each child, photocopy the heart box pattern and the accordion-fold letter to parents explaining the mission project. You may want to use colored copy paper for the box.

SAY: This is a special box because when you assemble it, the top of the box forms a heart. The heart reminds us that we are called to love our neighbors, no matter where they are.

- Have the children cut out the box on the solid lines. Fold inward on the dotted lines until it fits together.

- Let them add the "Love your neighbor" sticker to the back side of the box.

- Guide the children in cutting out the letter to parents, taping the strips in order, and folding the letter accordion-style.

- Insert the letter into the box and interlock the heart, as shown.

Good

Worship

Gather and Sing

Supplies: Bible Story Pak Songbooks, CD-ROM, CD player, "Keepers of the Flame Torches" (see p. 88)

Hands

- Have the children stand in a circle.

- Play the song "Keep the Faith" (Track #4) through one time.

SAY: We've talked about a "new life" through Jesus. We've learned about a "new Paul." Today we will be learning about the "new believers." If you've ever wondered what happened to Jesus' followers after his death and Resurrection, those are the stories we will be hearing. These followers didn't let the faith die. They kept it going and going and going and going until it came down to you.

- Hand out the songbooks. Read through the words with the boys and girls.

God

- Have the children pass their torches around the circle in rhythm as the song plays again. Place the torches under the chairs and save them until next week.

- Then teach the children the sign language for *good*, *hands*, and *God* (see page 91).

- Play the song again. Use these signs in the song where the words are sung.

SAY: Now we are the keepers of the faith, passing along what Jesus taught.

Praise and Respond

Supplies: Bible, Bible Story Pak Songbooks, Resource Pak—pp. 9 (bottom), 16, & 22, CD-ROM or DVD, CD player or DVD player, envelope, tape, world map or globe

🕐 Display the Unit 3 Bible Story Poster Base. Remove the pictures for Sessions 10-13. Locate the story picture for Session 10 (*Jesus' early followers gathered around a table to eat*). Store the rest in an envelope for later sessions. Display the Mission Poster in the worship area.

- Locate "True Believers" (Track #3) on the CD-ROM or DVD. Play it through one time. Have the children listen for things that describe "true believers."

- Read the words through one time with the children.

- Have the children link arms and sway to the left and right as the song plays again.

SAY: As "true believers," we are part of God's plan. We work together hand in hand. We are trying to make the world a better place.

- Remind the children of the mission project for this quarter. Point out the pictures of the children and adults of the Kamina Project on the Mission Poster. Locate Africa and the Democratic Republic of the Congo on a map or globe.

SAY: We are working hand in hand with the people of the Kamina Project to make their world a better place.

- Invite one of the children to read Acts 4:32.

- Then have one of the children place the picture from today's story on the Bible Story Poster with tape.

PRAY: Dear God, we thank you for these first Christians. Because of them, we know about Jesus today. We thank you for their bravery and their faithfulness. We thank you that they supported one another and helped one another just as Jesus taught. Help us to love and support one another just as they did. Amen.

TIP

Remind the children to take home their Good Neighbor Boxes with the letter to their parents. Set up a collection container for next week.

Plan for Next Week

The Same and Different (p. 94): Photocopy Reproducible 11a for every two children.

It's All Good (p. 96): Set out a variety of old magazines that contain pictures of people and animals. Write "All that God created is good" across the top of a piece of posterboard.

A Mother's Day Greeting (p. 97): Photocopy Reproducible 11b for each child. Photocopy Reproducible 11c on red copy paper for each child. You will also need several shallow lids into which you can pour black poster paint.

Peter and Cornelius

Bible Verse
The community of believers was one in heart and mind. (Acts 4:32)

Bible Story
Acts 10:1-28

Leap of Faith
As a Christian, I am called to care for others.

Before You Begin

The story of Peter and the Roman centurion Cornelius made a big impact on the religious community of their time. Up until then, by religious law, the Jewish and Gentile communities had to stay completely separate. There was to be no intermingling. They didn't socialize, and they didn't eat together. This was lived out with varying degrees of strictness, however, depending on where one lived.

In many regions, particularly those with large Gentile populations, some Gentiles even participated in the religious activities of the Jewish community, including attending the synagogue. These people were known as "God-fearers." If you remember, we encountered such a God-fearer in the story of Paul and Lydia.

Cornelius was also one of these "God-fearers." He participated in the prayers of the community and gave to the poor. He was regarded as a righteous, upstanding man. But Cornelius was never converted to Judaism. He had heard the stories about Jesus, however, and one day he had a vision. An angel told him to send for Peter, which he did. He knew that Peter was one of Jesus' inner circle of disciples. While the emissaries were on their way to Joppa to find Peter, Peter himself had a vision from God. Through this vision God was saying to him, "Nothing that God created is unclean—no food, no person." Because of this encounter, one of the major barriers to the faith came tumbling down.

The idea of eating or not eating certain foods because they are "clean" or "unclean" probably won't make much sense to the children. But they can understand what God was saying to Peter—all persons are equal in God's sight. God did not allow for exceptions. This concept is a difficult thing for many children (and many adults) because it means God loves the class bully just as much as God loves them. God may not like what the bully is doing, but that child is still God's creation and is just as precious to God. Our society today has different notions of what it means to be "unclean." Reinforce the idea that we are all God's children, loved by God without exception.

Session 11
May 12

TIP

Visit *GrowProclaimServe. com/leaders* to join the community with other leaders and find helpful weekly content and articles.

Requires preparation.

Grow Together

Choose one or more of the following activities to do as the children arrive.

Welcome the Children

Supplies: Resource Pak—pp. 2 & 23, Stickers, CD-ROM, CD player, offering basket, collection container for mission contributions

🕐 Display the attendance chart from the Resource Pak.

- Play "True Believers" (Track #3) and "Keep the Faith" (Track #4) as the children come into the room.

- Greet the children as they arrive.

- Show the children where to place their offerings and contributions to the Kamina Project.

- Give each child the attendance sticker for today to place on the chart.

Fun Pak Fun

Supplies: Fun Pak—p. 25, scissors, drawing paper, glue sticks, crayons or markers

- Let the children complete the four pictures, then invite them to share their completed images. Comment on how each person interpreted the picture in a different way, even though the starting image was the same.

Just for Fun

Supplies: Bible Story Pak—p. 3, pencils

- Remove the sheets for May 12 from the Bible Story Pak. Give the children the Just for Fun page.

- Have the children "go fly a kite!" They will match the kites that are the same.

The Same and Different

Supplies: Reproducible 11a, solid colored fabric or paper, 2 plastic forks and 1 spoon

🕐 Photocopy the worksheet for each pair of children.

ASK: *(Hold up a solid colored piece of fabric or paper.)* **Who has on the same color as the fabric/paper I'm holding up? Stand up if you do. Who is wearing a color that is different from the fabric/paper I'm holding up? Stand up.** *(Hold up two plastic forks.)* **Are these the same or are they different?** *(They're the same.)* *(Hold up a plastic fork and a plastic spoon.)* **Are these the same or are they different?** *(They're different.)*

- Pair the children. Give each pair a copy of the worksheet.

- Have each pair come up with five ways they are alike and five ways they are different. For example, they may both like pepperoni pizza; they may both dislike strawberry ice cream.

- Give the children about five minutes to come up with their lists.

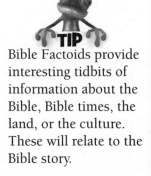

- Have the children bring their lists to the conversation area.

Conversation Time

Supplies: Birthday Celebration displays (see p. 8), tape, scissors, crayons or markers, "The Same and Different" lists (see p. 94)

- Have the children sit either in chairs or on the floor.

- Celebrate any birthdays that have occurred or will occur in the coming week. Use the birdhouse patterns and birthday grams.

ASK: What did each partner learn about the other person? (*Invite the partners to list things they had in common and things that were different.*) **Are the differences very different? Are the similarities very similar?**

SAY: Today we are going to hear a story about Peter. Who knows something about Peter? (*He was one of the twelve apostles. Peter was a fisherman when Jesus called him to be a disciple. Peter told people he didn't know Jesus when Jesus was arrested.*) **Something that Peter says and does in today's Bible story changed how Jewish Christians and other Christians treated one another.**

Proclaim the Word

Visit Leaper's Pointe

Supplies: DVD, DVD player

- The DVD is optional and can be used in place of "Interact With the Bible Story" or in addition to it.

- Place the DVD in the player. Locate Session 11.

- Invite the children to sit down where they can easily see the screen.

SAY: In today's story from Leaper's Pointe, Harley is upset. Coach Mondo won't let him play on the town baseball team because Harley is left-handed.

- Watch the DVD segment.

Interact With the Bible Story

Supplies: Bible Story Pak—p. 1

SAY: You would have thought by now that Peter would "know it all." After all, he had been one of Jesus' special twelve. He had traveled with Jesus for three years, learning everything he could. He was even one of Jesus' best friends. But he learned a new lesson today.

- Assign the parts and present the story from the Bible Story Pak.

All About the Story

SAY: A Gentile was anyone who wasn't Jewish. As far as the Jewish people were concerned, Jews and Gentiles did not mix. If a Jewish person came in contact with a Gentile, that person was considered unclean. This was avoided at all costs. Even when traveling, Jewish people carried their own food with them so they would not be contaminated by "Gentile food." They even carried hay for their donkeys and cattle for the same reason. It was serious separation.

ASK: Why did Cornelius, a Roman centurion and obviously a Gentile, send for Peter? (*He was told in a vision to do this.*) While his servants were traveling, what happened to Peter? (*Peter had a vision, as well.*) What did Peter's vision tell him? (*That nothing God created is unclean—not animals, not people.*) How would this change how the Jewish Christians felt about the Gentile Christians? (*There was no reason for separation anymore.*)

SAY: When Peter, a disciple of Jesus, went into Cornelius's house, it changed everything. No longer would Christians have to avoid each other because they were either Jewish or Gentile.

Bible Connection

Supplies: Bible Story Pak—p. 4, pencils

- Have the children write the first letter of the name of each animal in the appropriate box. They will discover what Peter learned in today's story. The children may need help identifying some of the more specific animals, such as number 14 (*iguana*) and 17 (*orangutan*). (*Answers on page 126.*)

It's All Good

Supplies: old magazines, posterboard, scissors, marker, glue sticks

🕐 Set out a variety of old magazines that contain pictures of people and animals. Write "All that God created is good" across the top of the posterboard.

- Have the children cut out pictures of people and animals and glue them to the posterboard.

SAY: Jesus' followers were out in the world, sharing the good news. At first they could only be around certain people. But when Peter visited Cornelius, a Roman centurion, they learned that everyone and everything God created is good.

Serve in Love

Kid Connection

Supplies: Bible Story Pak—p. 2, world map or globe

ASK: Who is our neighbor? Is (*name one of the children*) our neighbor? Is (*name the pastor of your church*) our neighbor? Is your teacher at school your neighbor? Are the boys and girls who live in Kamina your neighbors?

SAY: Everyone and everything that God created is good. God wants all people to have what they need—food, water, shelter.

- Talk with the children about the pictures in the Bible Story Pak.

- Locate the Democratic Republic of the Congo on the globe or world map.

- Talk about how Africa may seem far away, but in today's world, it is very close.

- Read about the lowland gorilla that lives in this country.

SAY: The money that we collect this month will go toward helping the people of Kamina have clean water, good food, a good education, and all the little things we take for granted.

A Mother's Day Greeting

Supplies: Reproducibles 11b & 11c, scissors, glue sticks, red copy paper, tape, paper punches, paper fasteners, black poster paint, shallow lids, hand-cleaning supplies, black markers

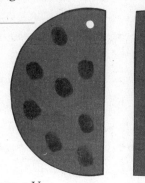

🕐 Photocopy the ladybug body and legs for each child. Photocopy the ladybug wings on red copy paper once per child. Pour a small amount of black poster paint into several lids, one lid for each two or three children.

SAY: Today is Mother's Day, a day set aside to tell our mothers how special they are. Let's make a card that we can share with them.

- Have the children cut out the ladybug body and legs. Punch a hole at the X. Tape the legs to the back side of the body, three on each side.

- Cut out the antennae strip and color it black on the back side. Fold it into a V shape, and then glue it to the back side of the ladybug's head.

- Cut out the wings. Punch holes at the X's. Overlap the holes and attach the wings to the body using a paper fastener.

- Add spots to the ladybug wings by pressing a finger into black poster paint and touching the wings. Add as many or as few spots as desired.

- Have the children take home their Mother's Day greetings today.

Worship

Gather and Sing

Supplies: Bible Story Pak Songbooks, CD-ROM, CD player, "Keepers of the Flame" Torches (see p. 88)

- Have the children stand in a circle.

- Play the song "Keep the Faith" (Track #4) through one time.

SAY: Last week we learned about those first Christians who came together to support one another and help one another. Today we heard about Peter and how what he did changed the way those first Christians came together.

- Hand out the songbooks. Read through the words with the boys and girls.

- Have the children pass their torches around the circle in rhythm and sing along as the song plays again. Then place the torches under the chairs.

- Review the sign language for *good*, *hands*, and *God* (see page 98).

- Play the song again. Use these signs in the song where the words are sung.

SAY: Now we are the keepers of the faith, passing along what Jesus taught.

TIP

Let the children take home their "Keepers of the Flame" Torches after today's service.

Praise and Respond

Supplies: Bible, Bible Story Pak Songbooks, Unit 3 Bible Story Poster Base and Pictures (see p. 92), **Mission Poster** (see p. 92), **CD-ROM or DVD**, CD player or DVD player, tape, world map or globe

Good

🕐 Locate the story picture for Session 11 (*Peter and Cornelius*).

- Locate "True Believers" (Track #3) on the CD-ROM or DVD. Play it through one time. Have the children listen for things that describe "true believers."

SAY: At first "true believers" believed that Jesus' message was only for the people who were Jewish. In today's story, they learned something new. Jesus' message is for all people.

- Read the words through one time with the children.

- Have the children link arms and sway left and right as the song plays.

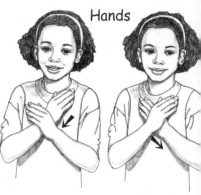
Hands

SAY: As "true believers," we are part of God's plan today. We know that all people are invited to be a part of God's family, no matter who they are.

- Remind the children of the mission project for this quarter. Point out the pictures of the children and adults of the Kamina Project on the Mission Poster. Locate Africa and the Democratic Republic of the Congo on a map or globe.

- Invite one of the children to read Acts 4:32. Have one of the children place the picture from today's story on the Bible Story Poster with tape.

PRAY: Dear God, we thank you for these first Christians. We thank you for Cornelius, who wanted to learn about Jesus. We thank you for Peter, who learned that God's love is for everyone. Thank you. We are all children of God, precious and loved. Amen.

God

Plan for Next Week

Conversation Time (p. 101): Make one copy of **Reproducible 12a** and use it to create a pinwheel from red paper.

Gone With the Wind (p. 102): Write each word of the Bible verse (Acts 4:32) on a different index card. You will need one card per child, and it's okay to have duplicates. Cut red crepe paper into 24-inch streamers. Bundle three or four together and tape at one end. Each child will need two bundles of streamers.

A Pentecost Windcatcher (p. 103): Photocopy **Reproducible 12b** for each child. Cut red, orange, and yellow art tissue into 1-inch by 18-inch strips. Use a paper cutter, cutting through several thicknesses, to make the job go faster. Each child will need about ten strips.

Praise and Respond (p. 104): Separate the "I Will Serve Today" cards (**Resource Pak—p. 20**). Tape each card to a separate sheet of colored paper. Arrange the papers in a circle around the worship center. Add blank sheets if you have more than twelve children, until there are enough spaces for all the children to stand. Add a loop of tape to the back of each sheet of paper to keep it in place.

TIP

Remind the children to bring in their money for the Kamina Project. May 26 will be the last Sunday to collect it.

GROW • Proclaim • Serve • Middle Elementary Leader's Guide

Pentecost

Bible Verse

The community of believers was one in heart and mind. (Acts 4:32)

Bible Story

Acts 2:1-41

Leap of Faith

As a Christian, I am called to care for others.

Before You Begin

The story of Pentecost is one of the most important stories of the church included in the Bible. Pentecost (actually the Jewish Festival of Weeks) is held fifty days after Passover. Jesus' disciples were waiting in Jerusalem for whatever it was Jesus had promised would come to them. Suddenly, in that upper room, they heard "a sound from heaven like the howling of a fierce wind," and they saw "individual flames of fire alighting on each one of them." This shared experience made them aware of the new inward power that would change them—and the world—forever.

For Christians, the Jewish festival now took on a new meaning. The disciples were no longer students, for they were now the conveyers of the message of Jesus and the power of the Resurrection. Peter stood outside the place where it all happened and told the world about the Resurrection, its power, and what it meant for the people who believed. Three thousand people were converted to Christianity that day. The new church was born.

Wouldn't it be nice if there were a simple way to explain the Holy Spirit—not just to the children, but to all of us? We can't see or touch the Holy Spirit, and yet we know that God is with us. We can see the Holy Spirit at work in the world. We can feel the Spirit at work in our lives. We can sense the presence of God because of the comfort and guidance that God provides for us through the Holy Spirit. But of all the things we learn as Christians, the Holy Spirit is probably the hardest to grasp and to explain to children.

We know the Spirit as surely as we know our names. But how do we explain an abstract concept to the children, who are very concrete thinkers? That falls to the writers, editors, and teachers who provide the words and experiences that will introduce the Holy Spirit. The children will encounter the Spirit on their faith journey. In fact, who's to say that the children themselves have not already felt the Spirit and just didn't know how to put it into words? When Jesus asked us to become like little children in our faith, he was asking us to trust even the things we don't understand. That is what faith is all about.

TIP

Visit *GrowProclaimServe. com/leaders* to join the community with other leaders and find helpful weekly content and articles.

Requires preparation.

Grow Together

Choose one or more of the following activities to do as the children arrive.

Welcome the Children

Supplies: **Resource Pak—pp. 2 & 23, Stickers, CD-ROM,** CD player, offering basket, collection container for mission contributions

---

🕐 Display the attendance chart from the Resource Pak.

• Play "True Believers" (Track #3) and "Keep the Faith" (Track #4) as the children come into the room.

• Greet the children as they arrive.

• Show the children where to place their offerings and their contributions to the Kamina Project.

• Give each child the attendance sticker for today to place on the chart.

Fun Pak Fun

Supplies: **Fun Pak—p. 27,** scissors, glue sticks

• Have the children assemble their flaming wind walkers, and give them an opportunity to toss them into the air to see what happens.

Just for Fun

Supplies: **Bible Story Pak—p. 3,** crayons or markers

• Remove the sheets for May 19 from the Bible Story Pak. Give the children the Just for Fun page.

• Have the children color the spaces as indicated in the directions. A flame for Pentecost will appear. *(Answer on page 128.)*

Go Fly a Plane

Supplies: colored copy paper, crayons or markers

• Invite the children to decorate a sheet of paper in any way they choose.

• Then have them fold the paper into a paper airplane shape. Any child who doesn't know how to do this can learn from someone else who does.

• Have an airplane flying contest to see whose airplane can travel the farthest.

ASK: What determines how far a paper airplane will travel? *(weight and lift)* **What causes the airplane to fall?** *(gravity)* **What causes the airplane to stay up?** *(air)* **Can you see air?** *(No.)* **Can you feel it?** *(when it's moving)*

SAY: Air passing over the wings of your plane caused it to stay up. Gravity pulling down on the plane caused it to come to the ground. When the lift caused by the air and the weight of the plane are equal, then the airplane stays up and travels straight. But when one is unequal to the other, the plane either goes up or comes crashing down. This is how real airplanes work, too.

TIP

If the wind walker has a tendency to "flop" rather than "walk," try adding a small paper clip at the bottom of the flame.

ASK: Can you see air? *(No.)* How do you know it's there? *(You can see what air does.)* When have you seen air at work? *(Let the children talk about times they've experienced air at work—such as storms, flying kites, hot air balloons, and so on.)*

SAY: Today we are going to learn about something else you can't see but that you know is there because you can see it at work.

Conversation Time

Supplies: Reproducible 12a, Birthday Celebration displays (see p. 8), tape, scissors, crayons or markers, red paper, ball-head straight pin, unsharpened pencil

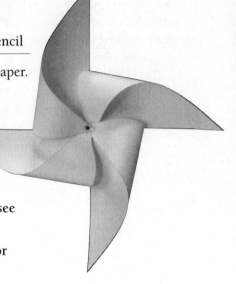

🕐 Make one copy of the pattern and use it to create a pinwheel from red paper.

- Have the children sit either in chairs or on the floor.

- Celebrate any birthdays that have occurred or will occur in the coming week. Use the birdhouse patterns and birthday grams.

- Blow the pinwheel and make it go around. Wave the pinwheel through the air causing it to spin. Let the children blow the pinwheel.

ASK: What makes this pinwheel spin? *(air)* How do you know? Can you see air? Can you touch air? Can you hear air? *(only when it's moving)*

SAY: Today we are going to hear about something else that you can't see or hear, but there is no doubt when it's there.

Proclaim the Word

Visit Leaper's Pointe

Supplies: DVD, DVD player

- The DVD is optional and can be used in place of "Interact With the Bible Story" or in addition to it.

- Place the DVD in the player. Locate Session 12.

- Invite the children to sit down where they can easily see the screen.

SAY: It's "Celebrate-the-Wind Day" in Leaper's Pointe, and things are really blowing around! There are bubbles, banners, balloons, kites, pinwheels, wind chimes, streamers, and flags. Merrilee explains that not only is this the time that Leaper's Pointe celebrates the wind, it's also the time that Christians celebrate Pentecost.

- Watch the DVD segment.

Interact With the Bible Story

Supplies: Bible Story Pak—p. 1

SAY: Before Jesus left the earth and went to be with God, he told his friends that they were to stay in Jerusalem and wait for the "helper" God would send to them. They must have wondered what or who this helper would be. But they waited. In today's Bible story, the waiting is over.

- Assign the parts and present the story from the Bible Story Pak.

All About the Story

SAY: Everyone was already in Jerusalem to celebrate the Festival of Pentecost—a spring harvest festival. They had gathered together in an upper room of a house in the city when it all happened.

ASK: What was the first thing they noticed? *(a fierce wind)* What was the second thing they noticed? *(There were flames of fire above each person there.)* What was the third thing that happened? *(Everyone began to speak in different languages—languages they had never spoken before.)* What did the people outside in the street think was going on? *(They thought there was a wild party going on.)* What did Peter tell them had happened? *(The Holy Spirit had come to each of them.)* What did Peter do then? *(He told the people about Jesus.)*

SAY: That day, thousands of people became believers in Jesus and were baptized.

Bible Connection

Supplies: Bible Story Pak—p. 4, Stickers

- Have the children fill in the blanks about the story using their sticker words. *(Answers on page 126.)*

Gone With the Wind

Supplies: index cards, red crepe paper, scissors, rulers, masking tape, marker

🕐 Write each word of the Bible verse (Acts 4:32) on a different index card. Each child will need one card. Cut red crepe paper into 24-inch streamers. Bundle three or four together and tape at one end. Each child will need two bundles of streamers.

- Tape a word to each child. Have them stand across the room with their streamers.

- Read the Bible verse, leaving out one of the words.

- When you finish and say "go," the child or children wearing the missing word will run across the room, letting the streamers flutter in the breeze.

- Play again, leaving out a different word each time, until all the children have had a chance to run across the room.

> **TIP**
> If you have a small group, choose only the main words from the Bible verse: *community, believers, one, heart,* and *mind.* With a large group you can have duplicate words.

Serve in Love

Kid Connection

Supplies: Bible Story Pak—p. 2, world map or globe

SAY: When Jesus left his friends here on earth, he promised to send them a helper. The Holy Spirit is that helper. The Spirit inspired them and guided them from that day forward. The Spirit strengthened them in what they were called to do, and the Holy Spirit does the same for us today. The Spirit helps us do the right thing, comforts us when we're sad, and strengthens those who

believe in Jesus Christ. Whenever we work for the good of God's people—
wherever they are in the world—then we are being powered by the Holy Spirit.

- Talk with the children about the pictures on the Bible Story Pak page.
- Locate the Democratic Republic of the Congo on the world map or globe.
- Talk about how Africa may seem far away, but in today's world, it is very close.
- Read about the forest elephant that lives in this country.

SAY: The money that we collect this month will go toward helping the people of Kamina have clean water, good food, and a good education. This money will be the Holy Spirit in action.

A Pentecost Windcatcher

Supplies: Reproducible 12b, scissors, glue sticks, art tissue (red, orange, and yellow), paper punches, paper cutter, string or yarn, crayons or markers, old file folders or cardstock, rulers

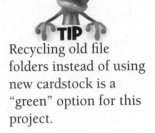

TIP
Recycling old file folders instead of using new cardstock is a "green" option for this project.

🕐 Photocopy the windcatcher pattern for each child. Cut art tissue into 1-inch by 18-inch strips. Use a paper cutter, cutting through several thicknesses, to make the job go faster. Each child will need about ten strips.

SAY: Today we will celebrate the wind and the Holy Spirit.

- Have the children color and cut out the dove and flame circles. Use one as a pattern to cut two circles from cardstock (or old file folders).
- Glue ten strips of the art tissue (a mixture of red, orange, and yellow) to the back of one of the cardstock circles along the bottom edge. (See photograph on the reproducible page.)
- Put glue on the back of the second cardstock circle and place it on top of the first circle, sandwiching the tissue strips inside.
- Glue the dove circle on one side and the flame circle on the other side.
- Punch a hole at the X and attach a piece of string or yarn for hanging.
- Remind the children that the dove and the flame are symbols of the Holy Spirit.

Good

Hands

Worship

Gather and Sing

Supplies: Bible Story Pak Songbooks, CD-ROM, CD player

God

- Hand out the songbooks. Read through the words for "Keep the Faith."
- Play the song "Keep the Faith" (Track #4) through one time.
- Review the sign language for *good*, *hands*, and *God*.
- Play the song again. Use these signs in the song where the words are sung.

SAY: Just like the disciples of long ago, we are now the keepers of the faith. Inspired by the Holy Spirit, we are called to pass along what Jesus taught.

Praise and Respond

Supplies: Bible, Bible Story Pak Songbooks, Resource Pak—p. 20, Unit 3 Bible Story Poster Base and Pictures (see p. 92), Mission Poster (see p. 92), CD-ROM or DVD, CD player or DVD player, colored paper, tape

🕐 Separate the "I Will Serve Today" cards. Each card represents either hands, feet, hearts, or voices. Tape each card to a separate sheet of colored paper. Arrange the papers in a circle around the worship center. Add blank sheets if you have more than twelve children, until there are enough spaces for all the children to stand. Add a loop of tape to the back of each sheet of paper to keep it in place. Locate the story picture for Session 12 (the disciples at Pentecost).

- Locate "True Believers" (Track #3) on the CD-ROM or DVD.

- Have each child stand on one of the paper squares. Play the song, and let the children walk around the circle.

- When you stop the music, have all the children who are standing on a picture say how in the coming week they can serve God using their hands, feet, hearts, or voices (depending on which picture they're standing on).

- Do this several times. Possible things might be: pray for someone, make someone a card, run errands for someone, offer to help someone, and so forth.

SAY: The faith is on the move! Inspired by the Holy Spirit, the followers of Jesus are ready to go into the world.

- Remind the children that next week is the last Sunday to collect money for the Kamina Project. Point out the pictures of the children and adults of the Kamina Project on the Mission Poster.

- Invite one of the children to read Acts 4:32. Have one of the children place the picture from today's story on the Bible Story Poster with tape.

PRAY: Dear God, we thank you for these first Christians. We thank you for Cornelius, who wanted to learn about Jesus. We thank you for Peter, who learned that God's love is for everyone. We thank you for the Holy Spirit who guides, comforts, and inspires us. Help us to be keepers of the flame. Amen.

TIP

Remind the children to bring in their money for the Kamina Project. May 26 will be the last Sunday to collect it.

Plan for Next Week

Welcome the Children (p. 106): Make several copies of Reproducible 13a. Cut out the fish symbols and tape them in discreet places in the room. These should be places where the children can work quietly, but they might also be under tables or in other unusual locations.

What's Your Name? (p. 106): Photocopy Reproducible 13b (code sheet) for each child. Cut off the bottom of each page and save for "Romans and Christians." Draw a fish symbol on a lunch-sized paper bag. Cut enough 3-inch by 9-inch strips of white paper for each child to have one.

Romans and Christians (p. 108): Make a copy of Reproducible 13b and cut apart the fish and soldier cards. Use more than one copy if you have more than nine children.

Next week is the last week to collect money for the mission project. Make any arrangements needed for delivering the money you've collected.

First Called Christians

Bible Verse

The community of believers was one in heart and mind. (Acts 4:32)

Bible Story

Acts 11:19-26

Leap of Faith

As a Christian, I am called to care for others.

Before You Begin

The new faith was spreading by "leaps and bounds." The persecution of Stephen had caused many of the believers to leave Jerusalem. When they left, they took with them their beliefs and the stories of Jesus, and they freely shared these things with the people they met along the way. Soon the faith was taking root among Gentile communities. A small Jewish sect was becoming a major religious movement with a great impact on the region.

As a small sect, the Roman government could ignore them and hope that they wouldn't cause any trouble. As a major religious movement and political force in the empire, the followers of Jesus became a threat to the stability of the Roman world. This would not be tolerated, and the Romans used every opportunity to discourage the Christians from practicing their faith. But the Christians, even in the face of great persecution, were undaunted.

The church in Antioch was one of the up-and-coming new congregations. A new ruling stated that a person didn't have to be a practicing Jew before becoming a follower of Jesus. This opened the church to a wealth of new believers, which is probably why Barnabas and Paul spent so much time with this active church. It was there in Antioch that the believers finally got a name—Christians. At first it was probably a term of derision, but the believers wore it with pride.

Names are important to children of this age. They may even resent another child having the same name they do. They will be annoyed when you mispronounce their names or, even worse, if you forget their names or call them by another name. Names are personal. For this reason, name-calling is a particularly hurtful thing to do. Your children may not yet understand the significance of the name *Christian*, but as they grow older, they will claim the name with pride.

TIP

Visit *GrowProclaimServe. com/leaders* to join the community with other leaders and find helpful weekly content and articles.

Requires preparation.

Grow Together

Choose one or more of the following activities to do as the children arrive.

Welcome the Children

Supplies: Resource Pak—pp. 2 & 23, Reproducible 13a, Stickers, CD-ROM, CD player, scissors, tape, offering basket, collection container for mission contributions

🕐 Make several copies of the fish symbols, cut them out, and tape them in discreet places in the room. These can be under a table, in a corner, or other unusual places. Display the attendance chart from the Resource Pak.

- Play "True Believers" (Track #3) and "Keep the Faith" (Track #4) at a low volume as the children come into the room.

- Greet the children with a whisper as they arrive.

SAY: *(whisper)* **We've got to be very quiet. We don't want the Roman soldiers to discover where we're meeting today.**

- Show the children where to place their offerings and their contributions to the Kamina Project.

- Give each child the attendance sticker for today to place on the chart.

Fun Pak Fun

Supplies: Fun Pak—p. 29, scissors, glue sticks, masking tape, colored duct tape, recycled newspaper, yarn or string, paper punches, rulers

- Have the children assemble their Bible verse fishing poles.

- Point out that the fish was a very important symbol for the early Christian church.

Just for Fun

Supplies: Bible Story Pak—p. 3, pencils

- Remove the sheets for May 26 from the Bible Story Pak. Give the children the Just for Fun page.

- Have the children find a place marked with the sign of the fish to work.

- Let the children try to find all the fish symbols in the illustration. *(Answers on page 128.)*

What's Your Name?

Supplies: Reproducible 13b (top), scissors, lunch-sized paper bag, 3-inch by 9-inch strips of white paper, marker, pencils

🕐 Photocopy the reproducible sheet for each child. Cut away the code section at the top. Each child will need a code sheet. (Save the rest of the page for "Romans and Christians.") Draw a fish symbol on a lunch-sized paper bag. Cut enough 3-inch by 9-inch strips of white paper for each child to have one.

- Have each child write his or her name on a strip of paper using the code. Encourage them to work in their "secret" places.

GROW • **Proclaim** • **Serve** • Middle Elementary Leader's Guide

- When the children have finished, have them place their names in the bag marked with the fish sign, and bring it to the conversation area.

Conversation Time

Supplies: Birthday Celebration displays (see p. 8), bag of names (see p. 106), name codes (see p. 106), tape, scissors, crayons or markers, dishpan or baking pan, sand, stick

It might be fun to meet under a table or in another secret place for today's conversation time.

- Fill the pan with sand and place it on the floor near the conversation area. Have the children sneak into the area, use the stick to draw a fish symbol in the sand, and sit down.
- Celebrate any birthdays that have occurred or will occur in the coming week. Use the birdhouse patterns and birthday grams.
- One at a time, draw a name out of the bag. Ask the children if they can figure out who it is using their name codes.

SAY: Everyone has a name. It's one of the ways we designate who is who. As more and more people became followers of Jesus, they were given a name, too. At first it was used to make fun of them. But Jesus' followers liked the name, and it stuck.

PRAY: We thank you, God, for the early Christians who told the stories of Jesus over and over again. We thank you that they carried the faith with them wherever they went. Amen.

Proclaim the Word

Visit Leaper's Pointe

Supplies: DVD, DVD player

- The DVD is optional and can be used in place of "Interact With the Bible Story" or in addition to it.
- Place the DVD in the player. Locate Session 13.
- Invite the children to sit down where they can easily see the screen.

ASK: How did you get your name? Were you named after a person in your family? A famous person? (*Let the children contribute.*)

SAY: Today in Leaper's Pointe, Merrilee is counting the suggestions for what to name the town's citizens. Mondo is sure his suggestion, Mondovians, will win, but Merrilee is not so sure. She remembers the trouble her Nana had trying to find a name for the townspeople. Merrilee thinks names are nice, but that what's inside matters more.

- Watch the DVD segment.

Interact with the Bible Story

Supplies: Bible Story Pak—p. 1, paper, marker

- Move to a different location marked with the sign of the fish.

ASK: How does it feel to have to sneak around and meet in secret places? Did you know that a long, long time ago, the followers of Jesus had to meet in secret, too? Do you know why?

SAY: The Romans, who ruled most of the world at this time, didn't much like the followers of Jesus. They thought that if they made life hard enough, Jesus' followers would disappear. They didn't disappear, but the followers of Jesus did decide to keep their activities secret. They used secret codes and secret symbols to mark their meeting places. The fish is one of these symbols. Anyone who saw this symbol knew that another believer was close by. The Greek word for fish is *ichthus.* *(Write this on a piece of paper, as shown.)* The Greek letters form an acrostic which represents the Greek words for "Jesus Christ, God's Son, Savior." That's why we use the fish symbol to identify ourselves as Christians.

> ι χ θ υ ς

- Assign the parts and present the story from the Bible Story Pak.

All About the Story

ASK: Why were the followers of Jesus leaving Jerusalem? *(It wasn't safe anymore.)* **Where did some of them go?** *(Antioch)* **Why?** *(Other believers had already gone there and formed a community.)* **Who did the church send to Antioch to help them?** *(Barnabas)* **What new name were the followers of Jesus given?** *(Christians)*

SAY: At first the name *Christian* was used to make fun of the followers of Jesus Christ. It means "little Christ." But later, people accepted the name with pride.

Bible Connection

Supplies: Bible Story Pak—p. 4, pencils

- Have the children follow each group of Christians to a new city, using each group's letters to fill in the blanks. The children will discover a secret message. *(Answers on page 128.)*

Romans and Christians

Supplies: Reproducible 13b (bottom), scissors, tape

- 🕐 Make one copy of the cards for every nine children. Cut them apart. (You may already have copies made from the "What's Your Name?" exercise.)

- Hold the cards face-down. Have each child take a card and tape it to the front of his or her body. If they draw a fish, they are Christians. If they draw a soldier, they are Romans.

- Designate a part of the room to be the "jail."

SAY: Not only did the Jewish leaders not like the followers of Jesus, but the Romans didn't either. The Roman emperor demanded that all citizens of the empire bow down and worship *him.* Of course the Christians weren't going to do this. This made them very unpopular with the Romans, and so they were tracked down and arrested.

- Romans will work together in pairs to surround a Christian. When a Christian is surrounded, he or she goes to "jail."

TIP

If you have a small group, select one child to be the Roman and let the other children be Christians. The Roman only has to tag the Christians.

GROW • Proclaim • Serve • Middle Elementary Leader's Guide

- When all the Christians are caught, the game is over. Let the children swap symbols and play again if there is time.

SAY: It was dangerous to be a Christian in those days. But aren't we glad they didn't get discouraged and give up?

Serve in Love

Kid Connection

Supplies: Bible Story Pak—p. 2, world map or globe

- Talk with the children about the pictures on the page and read the information. Read about the okapi that lives in this country.
- Locate the Democratic Republic of the Congo on the world map or globe.

SAY: Even though the people of Kamina are far away, and even though the animals that live in their country are different from the animals we see every day, we are still neighbors. We can still work together so that they can have clean water, good food, a good education, and a place to live—things God wants for all God's children.

Pendant Pride

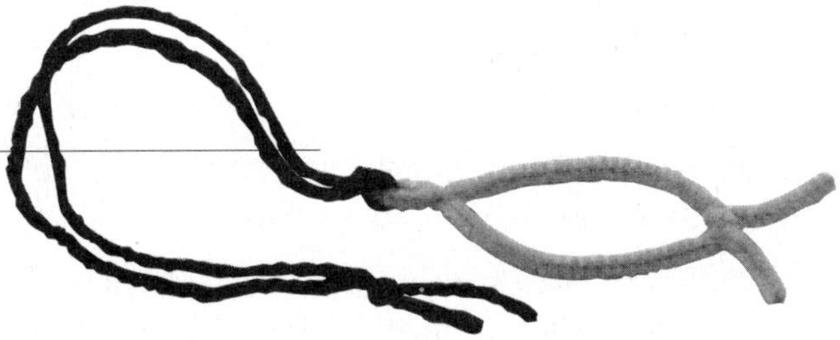

Supplies: chenille stems, yarn or ribbon

- Give each child a chenille stem. Have them fold it in half.
- Create a small loop at the top, as shown here.
- Shape the rest into the fish symbol.
- Attach yarn or ribbon to the loop using a larks head knot, as shown here.

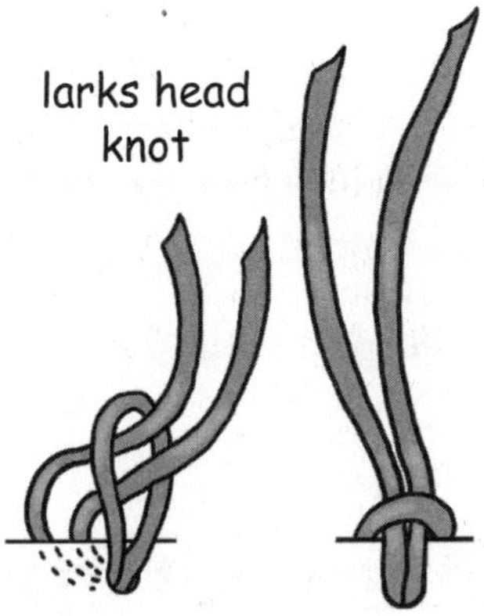

SAY: Today we can wear our faith with pride. We don't have to sneak around or use secret signs. We can announce it proudly. I am a Christian! (*Have the children repeat it after you several times, getting louder each time.*)

larks head knot

Worship

Gather and Sing

Supplies: Bible Story Pak Songbooks, CD-ROM, CD player

- Hand out the songbooks. Read through the words for "Keep the Faith."
- Play the song "Keep the Faith" (Track #4) through one time.
- Review the sign language for *good*, *hands*, and *God*, found on page 103. Then play the song again, using these signs in the song where the words are sung.

SAY: Just like the early Christians who were arrested and mistreated because of their beliefs, we are now the keepers of the faith.

Praise and Respond

Supplies: Bible, Bible Story Pak Songbooks, **Unit 3 Bible Story Poster Base and Pictures** (see p. 92), **Mission Poster** (see p. 92), **CD-ROM or DVD**, CD player or DVD player, "I Will Serve Today" squares (see p. 104), tape, collection container for mission contributions

🕐 Place the "I Will Serve Today" squares on the floor around the worship center (see p. 104). Locate the story picture for Session 13 (*the family traveling on the road*).

- Locate "True Believers" (Track #3) on the CD-ROM or DVD.

- Have each child stand on one of the paper squares. Play the song, and let the children walk around the circle.

- When you stop the music, have all the children who are standing on a picture say how in the coming week they can serve God using their hands, feet, hearts, or voices (depending on which picture they're standing on).

- Do this several times. Possible things might be: pray for someone, make someone a card, run errands for someone, offer to help someone, and so forth.

SAY: Because the followers of Jesus were faithful and brave, the stories of Jesus Christ, God's Son, the Savior, are told today. We are followers of Jesus just as those people were so long ago.

- Sing the song together.

- Place the mission collection container on the altar in the worship center.

- Read Acts 4:32. Have one of the children place the picture from today's story on the Bible Story Poster with tape.

SAY: We don't have to hide. We don't have to meet in secret. We do not have to worry about someone coming to arrest us and put us in jail. We can tell the good news openly and with pride.

PRAY: Dear God, we thank you for these first Christians who came together. We thank you for Cornelius, who wanted to learn about Jesus. We thank you for Peter, who learned that God's love is for everyone. We thank you for the Holy Spirit who guides, comforts, and inspires us. We thank you for those first Christians, who were brave and claimed their name. Help us to be keepers of the flame, too. Amen.

TIP

You may send the money for the Kamina Project to:

Advance GCFA, P.O. Box 9068, GPO, New York, NY 10087-9068.

If you are mailing a check, write in the memo line: "Kamina Orphanage, Advance #14398A."

Plan for Next Week

This is the end of the spring quarter. If you have received your materials for winter, scan the first session and make preparations. Please take time to fill out the survey on page 125 and send it in. Your comments will help us make a better resource for you and your kids.

GROW • **Proclaim** • **Serve** • Middle Elementary Leader's Guide

Reproducible 10a

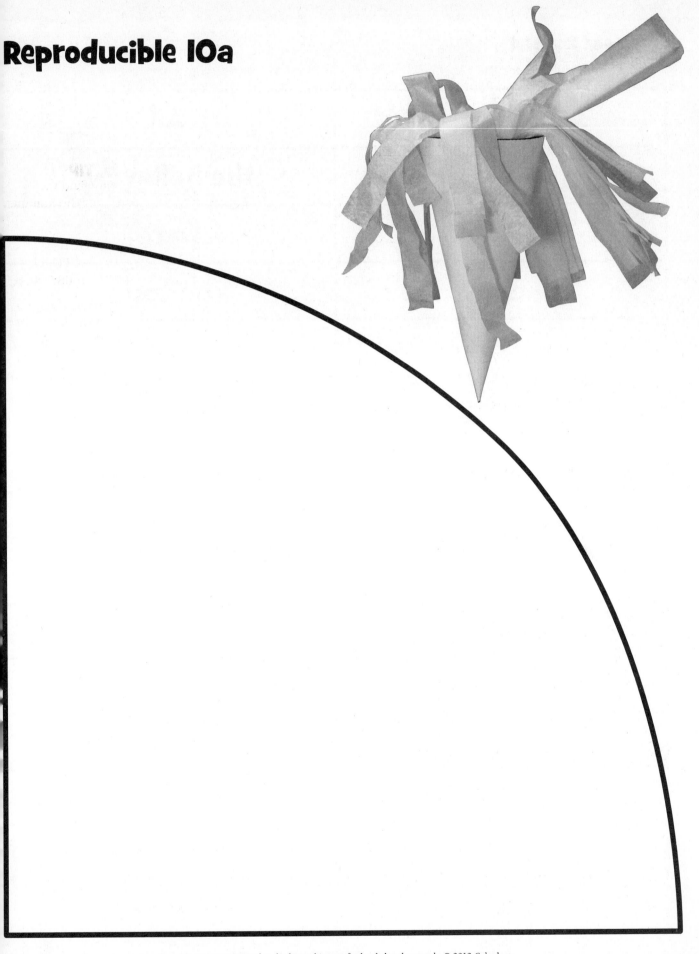

Reproducible 10b

There	All
were	the believers
no	were
needy	united
persons	and
among	shared
them	everything
Acts 4:34	**Acts 2:44**
The first word rhymes with "hair."	The first word has double letters in it.
The second word rhymes with "fur."	The second and third words have 4 "e's" in all.
The third word is a negative word.	The fourth word ends with an "e."
The fourth word means "very poor."	The fifth word means "joined together."
The fifth word means "human beings."	The sixth word rhymes with "sand."
The sixth word ends with a "g."	The seventh word begins with "sh."
The seventh word includes an "m."	The eighth word has 10 letters.

GROW • **Proclaim** • **Serve** • Middle Elementary Leader's Guide

Reproducible 10c

Dear Parents:

In the month of May, we are working together with other Grow, Proclaim, Serve boys and girls across our country to help fund the feeding program at the Kamina Children's Home.

In the mid and late 1990's, a

staggering number of children flooded into Kamina, DRC (Democratic Republic of the Congo). Due to the violence, disease, and poverty caused by the war, these children and thousands like them were orphaned. Often following the death of parents, children are taken in by other family members. Unfortunately, the

speed and quantity of children orphaned at this time were more than the community could absorb. Hundreds of children in Kamina alone were left without parents or any means of survival. In 1997, the United Methodist Church in the North Katanga District responded to this need by opening an orphaned

children's home. It began with one woman bringing six children into her home, and by 2000, it had become a full facility. Widowed women from the community cared for the forty children seen as being the most at risk.

Along with the children's home, the church worked

to place other children into homes in the community. Extended families agreed to take them in with the promise that the church, in partnership with UMCOR (United Methodist Committee on Relief), would help feed them. This was the start of the extended feeding program.

Last fall, construction was

completed that increased the capacity of the home to 160 children. Currently there are almost 50 children living in this facility, with many more who desire to be in the program. The goal this year is to increase that number as we secure commitments from churches in the United States to sponsor these and

additional children.

Recently a volunteer partnership began between the children's home and the members of the Kamina-Ville JPC (Young Adults for Christ). These volunteers are constructing a garden, playing soccer with the kids, and telling Bible stories in the evenings.

To help keep these severely overstretched new family units together, the North Katanga Conference and UMCOR (United Methodist Committee on Relief) partnered to start the external feeding program. About 500 children, selected based on need (orphans, children in single-parent homes, and other high-risk situations),

were fed multiple times per week thanks to this partnership.

With the coming of calm to the DRC, and of humanitarian disasters in other parts of the world, UMCOR shipments of food to Kamina have ended. The need, however, has not. In recent months, the external feeding program has suffered

dramatic cut-backs and even sporadic suspensions of operation. There is currently no sustainable funding source for this program. Finding one is among our top priorities.

The money collected by your church and churches all across the country will help to feed the children of this area. The boys and girls at Kamina

orphanage are our neighbors. We are called to love and share with them, just like the early church that your child has been learning about.

Annual Goal: $85,000
Location: DRCongo, Africa
Partner: The UMC, North Katanga Episcopal Area
Kamina Orphanage
Advance #14398A

TAPE TOP OF RECTANGLE "B" HERE   TAPE TOP OF RECTANGLE "C" HERE

Reproducible 10d

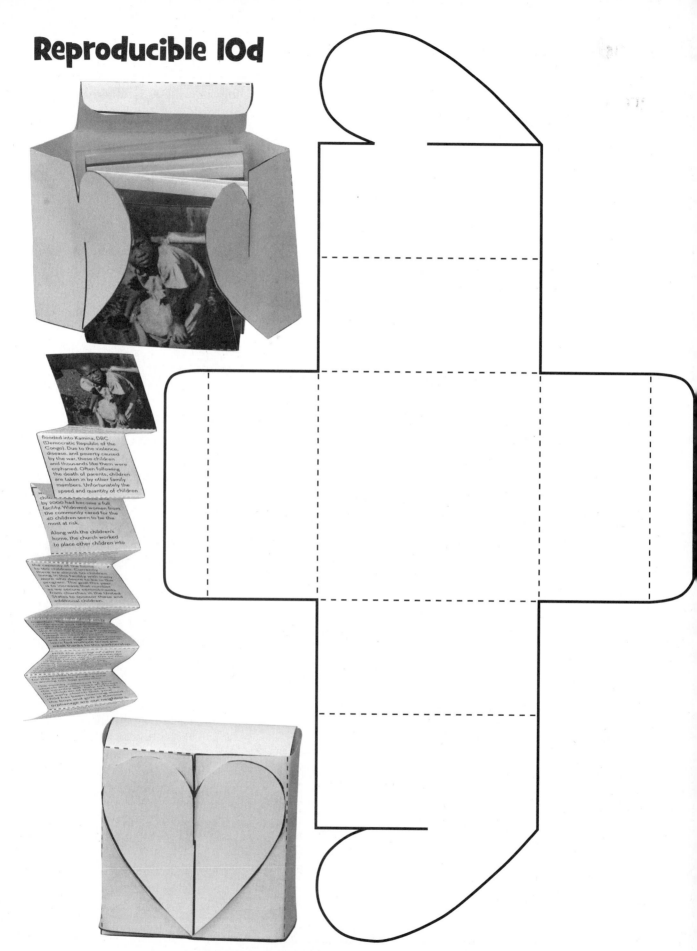

Reproducible 11a

We are the same in these five ways:

1.

2.

3.

4.

5.

We are different in these five ways:

1.

2.

3.

4.

5.

Reproducible 11b

X

This
ladybug
contains a hug
for your special day.
Mom, you're great!
Let's celebrate!
Happy Mother's Day!

Legs

Antennae: fold in half into a V shape

Reproducible IIc

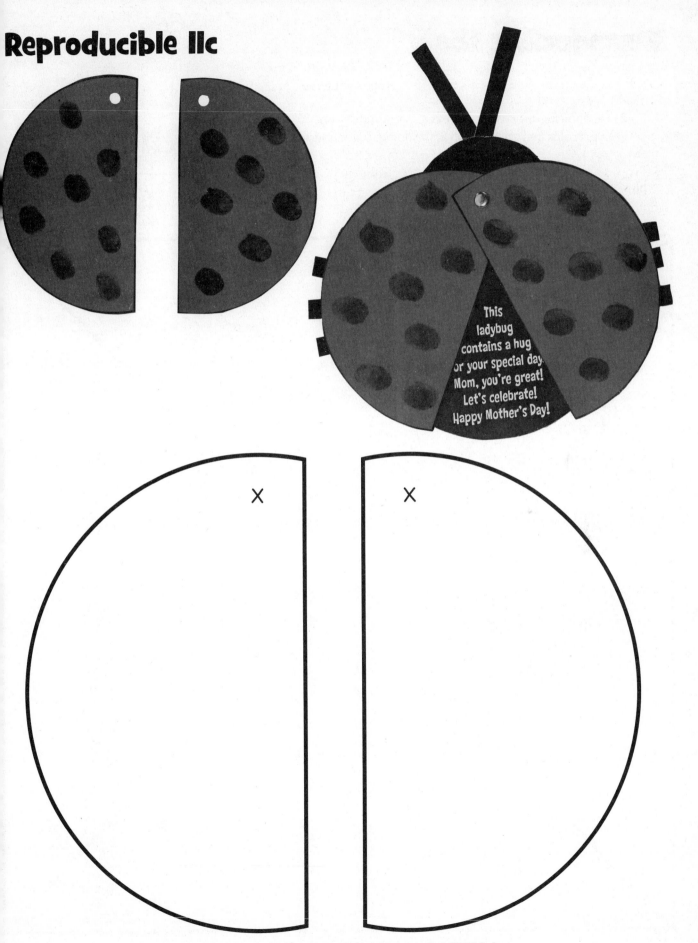

This
ladybug
contains a hug
for your special day.
Mom, you're great!
Let's celebrate!
Happy Mother's Day!

X   X

Reproducible 12a

1. Cut out the square, and cut slits from the corners along the solid lines
2. Fold every other corner (one side of each section that you cut) to the center, and secure them at the dot with a ball-head straight pin.
3. Press the pin into the eraser of an unsharpened pencil, and blow on the pinwheel to make it go around.

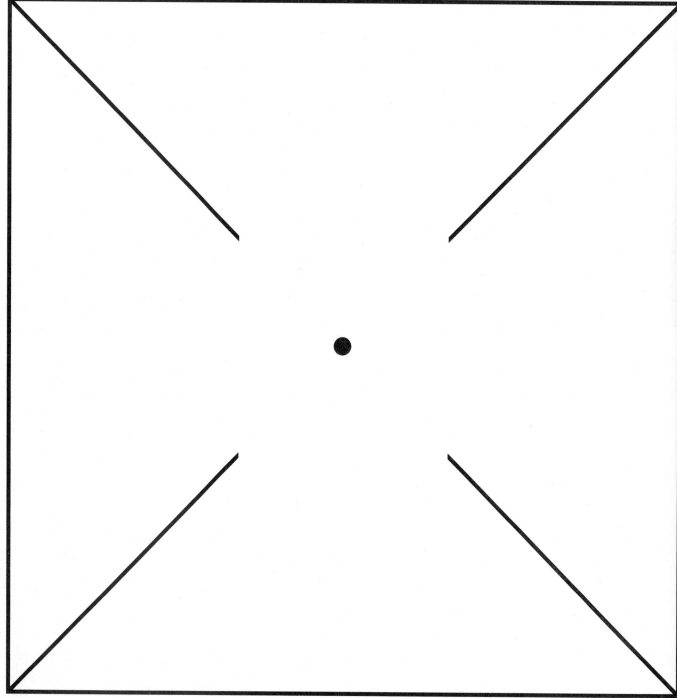

Reproducible 12b

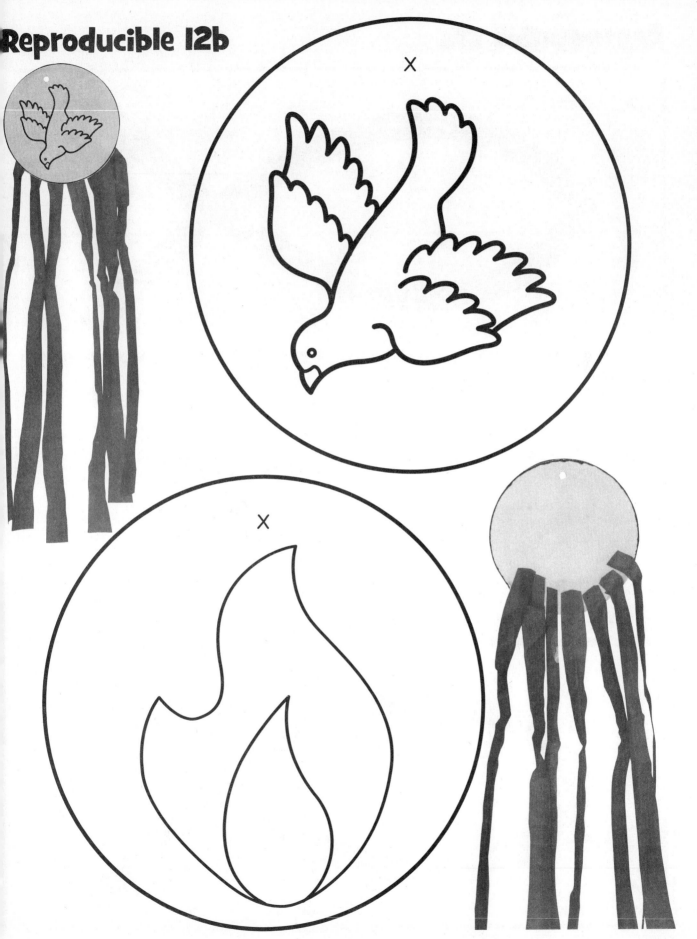

Reproducible 13a

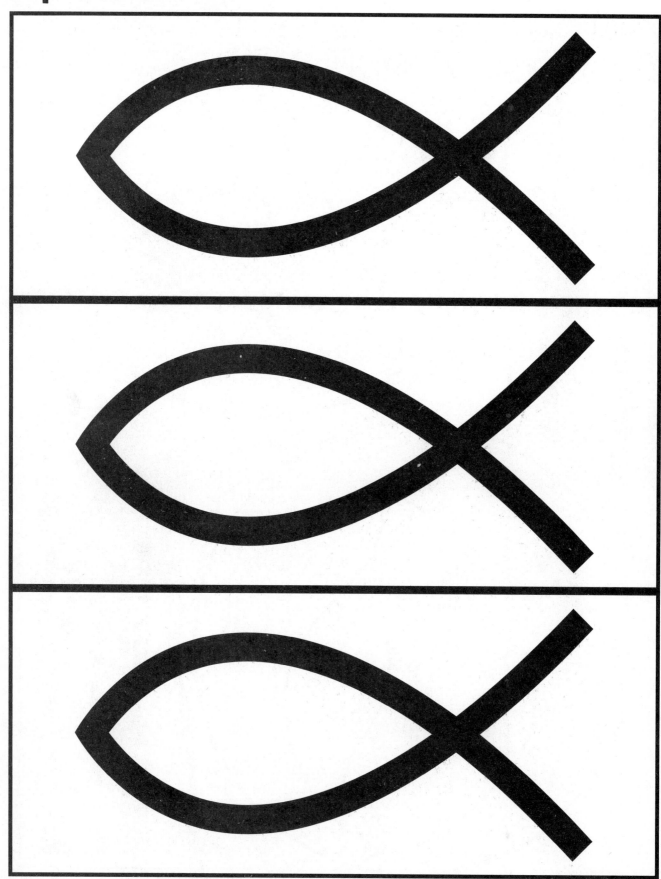

GROW • **Proclaim** • **Serve** • Middle Elementary Leader's Guide

Reproducible 13b

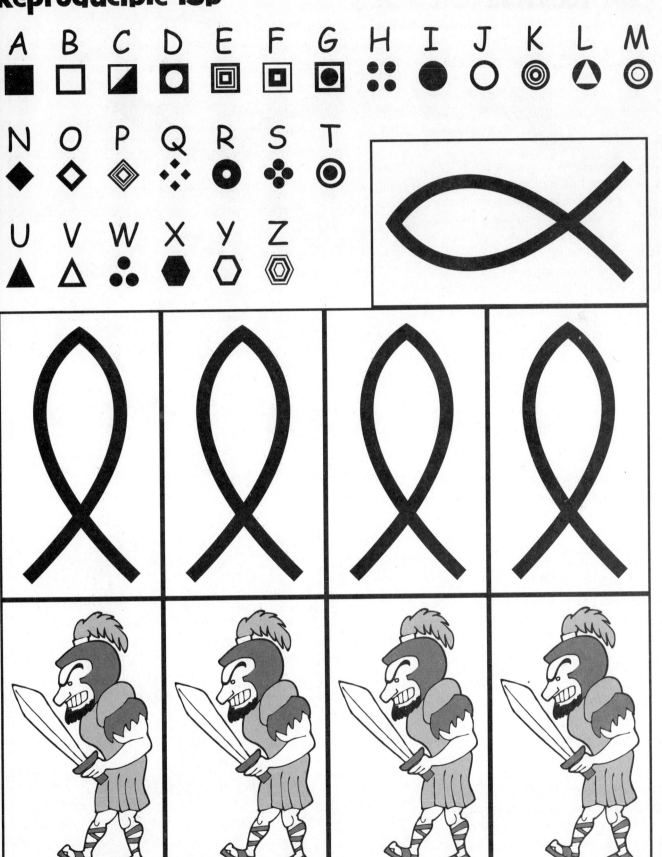

The New Life Cross

The cross is the most recognized symbol of Christianity. While the cross is the symbol of Jesus' death and suffering, the empty cross also represents the Resurrection—the triumph over death.

> "If anyone is in Christ, that person is part of the new creation."
> (2 Corinthians 5:17)

As Christians, we are an Easter people. Because God raised Jesus from the dead on that Easter morning, we are people of joy and hope. That is what we are trying to convey to the children with the "New Life Cross." The children will be seeing signs of "new life" in the world around them as the winter fades away into spring. We will be using some of these illustrations to help the children understand the new life we have in Jesus Christ.

The first unit of the spring quarter is called "New Life." It features the stories of Jesus' last week on earth. During this time, we want the children to see how they are called to grow in their faith and renew their commitments to being followers of Jesus. We will be using five living things that begin life as one thing and then change into something completely different—the frog, the chicken, the flower bulb, the peacock, and the butterfly. We will explain, however, that these are "outside changes." During Lent and Easter we are called to change on the inside.

Jesus himself said:
> "I am the resurrection and the life. Whoever believes in me will live, even though they die. Everyone who lives and believes in me will never die."
> (John 11:25-26)

The Resource Pak (p. 21) offers some options on how to make a "New Life Cross." Do not be limited by these options. Make the cross as simple or as complex as you feel suits your group of children. If you have a large Sunday school, your New Life Cross will be filled with images of new life by the end of March.

TIP

If you have a large class, you will need a large display space. The new life crafts are dramatic, and each child will want to make sure her or his symbol is displayed.

New Life Cross Symbols

Each age level will have the same symbols but will make them in a different way.

Session 1: the frog
Session 2: the egg and chick
Session 3: the daffodil flower
Session 4: the peacock
Session 5: the butterfly

GrowProclaimServe.com

Cloaks and Branches

1. Photocopy the pictures so that every pair of children will have one cloak and one branch.
2. Cut out each picture and glue it to a separate sheet of construction paper or scrap copy paper.
3. Follow the directions in the Leaders Guide (page 28) to play the game.

GROW • **Proclaim** • **Serve** • Middle Elementary Leader's Guide

1. Which resources do you use? (check all that apply)
   ☐ Leader's Guide
   ☐ Student Resources (Bible Story Paks)
   ☐ Fun Paks   ☐ Resource Pak
   ☐ Music CD-ROM / Music CD   ☐ DVDs
   ☐ Publicity Items (Banner, Postcard, and so forth)

2. Which quarter did you teach?
   ☐ Fall   ☐ Winter
   ☐ Spring   ☐ Summer

Use the following scale to rate each of the resources:

1 = NEVER   2 = SOMETIMES
3 = MOST OF THE TIME   4 = ALL THE TIME
N/A = NOT APPLICABLE

3. Leader's Guide
   ___ Easy to use
   ___ Used a variety of learning styles
   ___ Matched my current church situation
   ___ Bible story was central to the session

4. Student Pieces
   ___ Activities were fun for the kids
   ___ Art was appealing
   ___ Appropriate for the skill level of my boys and girls
   ___ Encouraged growth in Bible skills

5. Fun Paks
   ___ Creative activities that the children enjoyed
   ___ Clear and concise directions
   ___ Related to the faith experience of the session
   ___ Age-appropriate for the children

6. Resource Pak
   ___ Visually appealing to the children
   ___ Games were fun and easy to lead

7. Music CD-ROM / Music CD
   ___ Children enjoyed singing and moving to the music
   ___ Music related to the sessions

8. DVDs
   ___ Children enjoyed Leaper's Pointe
   ___ Children enjoyed the music and movement videos
   ___ The sign language of the Bible verse was helpful

9. What was your favorite activity this quarter?

10. What was your least favorite activity this quarter?

11. Tell us about one faith experience in your group this quarter.

12. Did you find enough material for the time you had available?
    Yes   No
    How much time did you have?
    Comment:

13. Did you see spiritual growth in your kids? (in prayer, eagerness about the Bible, their relationships with one another)
    Yes
    No

14. Any other comments?

15. How many children did you have in your group? _____

16. How many leaders did you have in your group for each age level that you taught? _____

17. What is the approximate membership size of your church?
    ☐ Under 100   ☐ 100–199   ☐ 200–299
    ☐ 300–499   ☐ 500–749   ☐ 750–999
    ☐ 1000+

18. In what area is your church located?
    ☐ Urban   ☐ Suburban
    ☐ Small town   ☐ Rural

Name: _____

Church Name: _____

Church Address: _____

City: _____

State: _____

ZIP: _____

E-mail Address: _____

Phone #: _____

Please return this form to:

The Children's Team
201 8th Avenue, South, P.O. Box 801
Nashville, TN 37202-0801

If you have additional questions or comments please contact:
Curric-U-Phone: 1-800-251-8591, Mon-Fri 8:00 am-4:00 pm CST,
or *Curricuphone@Cokesbury.com*.

Answers for the Bible Story Pak

Session 1, page 3:

Serve

Session 1, page 4:

John the Baptist, Jesus; Passover, Jerusalem, to eat, washed the disciples' feet, Peter, "Unless I wash you, you won't have a place with me."

Session 2, page 2:

Bethlehem, Mary, Joseph, Shepherds, Wise men, star, fishermen, God, live, Son, Christians

Session 3, page 4:

Jesus; Jesus; Peter, James, John; Jesus; Judas; Judas; Soldiers

Session 4, page 3:

Hosanna to the King!

Session 4, page 4:

Jerusalem (1), Passover (9), Jesus (2), donkey (8), branches (6), cloaks (3), road (4), Hosanna (7), King (5); Messiah

Session 5, page 3:

Jesus is alive!

Session 6, page 4:

1) jellyfish, 2) campfire, 3) sun, 4) light bulb, 5) fireflies; Jesus; "Saul, Saul, why are you harassing me?"

Session 7, page 3:

Escaped

Session 7, page 4:

traveled, arrest, blinded, met, changed, preached, angered, kill, climbed, lowered, escaped, preaching

Session 9, page 3:

Believe in Jesus

Session 10, page 3:

Everything; 1) egg, 2) vase, 3) elephant, 4) rooster, 5) year, 6) tree, 7) house, 8) icicle, 9) nest, 10) gorilla

Session 10, page 4:

They met together. They shared their meals. They prayed together. They praised God. They cared for one another.

Session 11, page 4:

All God created is good. 1) alligator, 2) lion, 3) lobster, 4) goat, 5) octopus, 6) dolphin, 7) camel, 8) raccoon, 9) elephant, 10) ant, 11) turtle, 12) eagle, 13) duck, 14) iguana, 15) spider, 16) giraffe, 17) orangutan, 18) otter, 19) deer

Session 12, page 4:

Pentecost, wind, room, flame, Holy Spirit, speak, crowd, wondered, Peter

GROW • Proclaim • Serve • Middle Elementary Leader's Guide

Answers for Bible Story Pak

▼ Session 2, Page 3

▼ Session 3, Page 3

▼ Session 5, Page 4

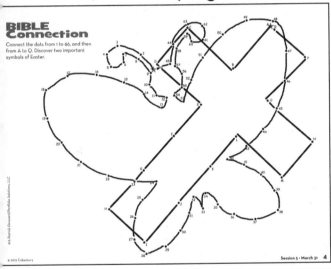

▼ Session 6, Page 3

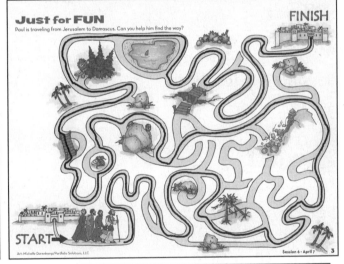

Answers for Bible Story Pak

▼ Session 8, Page 3

▼ Session 8, Page 4

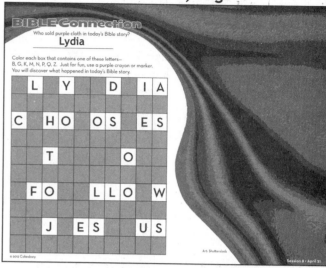

▼ Session 9, Page 4

▼ Session 12, Page 3

▼ Session 13, Page 3

▼ Session 13, Page 4

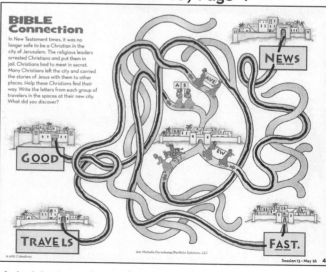